TABLE OF CONTENTS

Chapter 1: The necessary question 1
Chapter 2: The value of time 21
Chapter 3: The philosophy of time management today 36
Chapter 4: Have your goals written 64
Chapter 5: Don't start the day until you have it finished 90
Chapter 6: Eat a frog first 116
Chapter 7: Allocate time in categories 153
Chapter 8: Do things that have long term gratification 165
Chapter 9: Set up a finish line 174
Chapter 10: Law of 3 180
Chapter 11: Time is like capital; you can't let someone steal your seed coin 189
Conclusion: 206

CHAPTER 1
THE NECESSARY QUESTION

Learning how to deal with your time doesn't need to take a great deal of time. Time is a precious gift. At the point when you contribute it well, it's set apart with importance and exceptional moments of satisfaction. In any case, in case you're similar to such vast numbers of, you feel rushed.

Time Management Magic is tied in with learning a framework and a perspective that improves the capacity to lead a highly productive, adjusted, and effective life. Such a large number of individuals get discouraged and need to stop since they have setbacks and different obstructions throughout their life.

He credits his success to making some reliable time management system set up to guarantee he would do what he said he would do and stay successful in his obligations.

The official time management mysteries contained in Time Management Magic assist readers with monitoring all pieces of their lives and kick off their own and professional growth.

Time management is a learnable skill, and in this reexamined version, Morgenstern gives a definitive tool to join, delegate, and eliminate with unnecessary tasks; set innovation to work; and quit hesitating for the last time.

Her framework has helped countless readers reveal their psychological stumbling blocks and strengths, and build up a time-management that suits their individual needs.

Productive individuals don't attempt to do everything. They figure out how to concentrate on the most significant tasks and ensure those complete. They eat their frogs. There's a well-known axiom that if the primary thing you do every morning is to eat a live frog, you'll have the fulfillment of realizing you're finished with the most exceedingly bad thing you'll need to do throughout the day. For Tracy, eating a frog is an illustration for handling your most testing undertaking - yet also, the one that can have the best positive effect on your life. Eat That Frog! Tells you the best way to sort out every day so you can focus on these primary assignments and achieve them proficiently and successfully. The world has changed and how we work needs to change, as well. With wisdom from 20 leading creative minds, Manage Your Day-to-Day will give you a toolbox for handling the new difficulties of a day in and day out, consistently on the work environment.

This book presents a unique mix of the different moral, social, and mental parts of human life. The writer improves the book with many short; however, informative stories about the stream as a significant condition of the human mind. Besides, personal attitudes and specific terms will make the reader imagine that a genuine discussion with an expert analyst is happening through the lines of the book.

Reading this book isn't about instruction as it were. It is also about fun and collaboration between the author and the reader.

Time management:

Time management is the way toward organizing and planning events or tasks. It is the activity of conscious control over the measure of time spent on specific exercises, particularly with the end goal of expanding productivity, proficiency, or effectiveness. It has been a significant part of the business and projects the board for quite a while. However, it is progressively being applied to instruction and individual exercises in our busy, time-conscious current world. No less a figure than the influential administration advisor and author Peter F. Drucker once opined, "Time is the scarcest asset and except if it is managed nothing else can be managed."

We, as a whole, begin with a similar time. Everybody gets 24 hours per day in any case. What we do with our 24 hours throughout every day decides at last where we end up. How we utilize those 24 hours is our decision, when we see that every one of these 24 hours is a blessing, the entire thought of time management changes. With innovation available 24*7, the whole compartmentalization idea of individual and work life is never again substantial. We are associated with our messages all during that time, and we hardly switch off. As we have heard a million times, all-time administration specialists state we should browse messages 2-3 times each day. This is more difficult than one might expect, and by and by, I don't agree with this methodology. For a significant number of us, our work lives include email, and speed is the essence, particularly if your client or group needs something urgent.

I think the better method to manage email is to give it the regard it merits. Leaving unanswered email (I am discussing official email), which is significant, doesn't search high, and for a large portion of us, an aspect of our responsibilities described is to be responsive, and that gets admiration from others. I will conflict with what a large part of the specialist's state, yet my point is to be honest about what works for me. I do spend my initial 20 min in the wake of awakening, checking my email, and reacting to important things as relevant. I feel this holds me under tight restraints on to expect the rest of the day and leaves me less anxious when I arrive at work. Again this may not be material for everybody. I additionally get up ahead of schedule, so I do possess some energy for exercise or reading.

During my work hours, I am associated all through (obviously, there are exceptional cases with groups) and guarantee that I answer my messages rapidly and instantly as relevant. If you are working on a deliverable that requirements complete consideration, at that point by all methods, you can turn off from email for 2-3 hours before you check. You can set up automatic replies to show that you will search messages for that day just on specific occasions. You can also give a get back to the number for anything urgent. As I said, every day and every circumstance is extraordinary, so you must be adaptable in changing your arrangements for the afternoon.

Anyway, I ensure that any email I receive on my telephone works just when I open that mail application manually at the end of the day. I don't arrange notices which again improve a feeling of control. That is a similar way I handle Gmail, Twitter, Facebook, WhatsApp, and I don't set up any notifications. When I log in to the application, would I be able to see the notifications? This makes me feel that I am in charge. Therapists have additionally confirmed that a feeling of control is essential to like yourself. This additionally gives an enhanced sense that you are in charge of your time. In

Smarter Faster, Better, Charles Duhigg contends that people who have an internal locus of control experience higher self-inspiration and achievement. They also will, in general, gain more cash. Having an external locus of control relates to a higher pressure.

When I return home, I don't search for email for several hours and check again before resting. At last, I don't accept there is a single way to deal with time management, and there is no standard that you shouldn't check email before anything else or last thing at night. I do tune in to the experts at the end of the day; I choose what I need to do with my time and how that makes me feel like I am in control. So I urge you to think about what works best for you, and if you found what I shared valuable, you can take some part of it and incorporate it with your time management program. Again we need to choose what works best for us genuinely. Another approach to manage emails is to send a few emails, which imply we will also get lesser. At whatever point conceivable have a call or meet face to face to resolve disputes.

Some different quick ones on time management

1. Set clear objectives on what you need to achieve for a specific day or week. Think about the master plan at whatever possible as this will assist you with overcome short term setbacks faster. As of late, I went over the Resilient digital broadcast by having Mike Kearney Host of Deloitte Advisory's Resilient Podcast with Frank Tirelli, who was CEO of Deloitte Italy and CEO of Herb life International Inc. It was a captivating discussion, and he says each day he has a 3-page plan he takes a look at. It comprises what he should do each morning, his objectives in all aspects of his life, values, the things he is appreciative of, statements, and much more. The Resilient Podcast is a brilliant asset for all pioneers.

2. Keep up records on what should be finished. You can also plan exercises or tasks legitimately into your schedule. This is by all accounts the famous way now.

3. Another famous methodology is to concentrate on what must be accomplished for that day simply. This holds your tension under check. A decent book that I

preferred on time management is "How to Have a Good Day" via Caroline Webb.

4. When you complete a thing on the list, move it to the finished status, which makes you feel better.

5. Set aside some effort for yourself (it tends to be as less as 15 min) in the allotted 24 hours to achieve something you like. It tends to work out, sitting in front of the TV, walking, reading, or listening to music.

6. Once or more than once in a week, record in your diary what worked out in the right way in the week and what should be possibly better. You can also follow your achievements. Writing in a journal is a life-enhancing activity.

7. Always focus on doing the most significant assignment on your list first. This gives you the best profit for your speculation of time. In emergency clinics, patients are not treated regarding appearance yet are treated in terms of severity. Similar holds useful for the things on the list.

8. Guarantee 7-8 hours of rest by and large. At the point when you rest well, you are energized and can deal

with the tasks with substantially more excitement and energy.

9. Exercise again supports your energy, and once you get it off the beaten path toward the beginning of the day, it gives a feeling of achievement. The more pressure you have, the more you have to devote time to restoration. Indeed what I have found is to exercise regularly for any significant period, and it is a lot simpler to keep up the energy that way.

10. This is a bummer, however, worth repeating that when you are appreciative, you feel significantly more joyful and less upsetting. Take some time in a day to express sincere gratitude for everything great in your life. This puts the brain on appreciation, and it's challenging to be cranky when you are thankful. It additionally expands the satisfaction levels.

11. Jim Collins, the creator of Good to great, encourages us to utilize quit doing records. We all have to-do lists; however, he says you can be genuinely compelling just when you stop doing certain things that are draining your time and energy.

12. Figure out how to state no. We can't do everything, so it is fundamental that we evaluate our capacities and guarantee that we disapprove of things that will overpower us.

13. Truly desire is incredible; without it, a significant part of the advancement made would not have occurred. Anyway, it should be married with a pragmatic methodology implying that you need to guarantee that being excessively aggressive should not block your peace of mind. Ultimately peace of mind is a definitive objective.

14. Taking a break totally from technology on one day of the week is excellent and energizes you. I can't do it for a whole day, yet even a couple of hours without technology can be a good start. Padmasree Warrior takes this digital detox each Saturday. She says "I've taken Saturdays to be the day I pull back totally, I do things that are progressively imaginative, and I've really discovered that causes me when I get over into work to be more thoughtful, and I genuinely accept that feeding your creative soul is extremely critical to be more analytical."

Other Time Management Concepts

Time use research about is a creating field of study, and concerns how time is allotted over various exercises, for example, time spent at home, at work, shopping, traveling, etc. A few parts of the time utilize will, in general, be moderately steady over significant periods, for example, the measure of time spent traveling out to work. Different aspects, however, have changed significantly in current years as new technologies, for example, TV, cellphones, and the Internet, have made new chances to utilize time in various manners.

Time banking is a correlative cash framework created during the 1980s that viably utilizes time (for example an hour of any individual's work) as a unit of cash, in this manner giving a more literal interpretation to the frequently utilized expression "time is cash," first-authored by Benjamin Franklin as right on time as 1748. The thought is that time spent doing work that doesn't ordinarily give money related advantages (for example tutoring kids, thinking about the old, being neighborly, and so on) acquires "time" or "time dollars" that would then be able to be spent to get different services of various kinds. Timebanks have been built up in different countries around the world, yet it has not become a mainstream phenomenon.

Do you end up running at a much progressively furious pace during the Christmas season? I do. Along these lines, as I took a look at my endless plan for the day and cutoff times quick moving toward, I did a Google search on "time management." I got 1,610,000,000 query items. A lot of us are scanning for approaches to oversee time better. As I read through the different tips, I understood that our fixation on dealing with our schedules has brought about our schedules managing us. I understood that my point of view that I am time-starved is preventing me from being successful as a leader.

A large number of us are stuck in a viewpoint on how we deal with our time decides how viably we lead or how adequately we live our lives. This is what we're missing.

The Greek savants recognized time in two aspects: Chronos (chronological or schedule time) and Kairos (the ever-present "at this point"). "Kairos" as indicated by

Wikipedia is characterized as "a passing moment

when an opening shows up which must be passed through with power if the achievement is to be accomplished." presently starved point of view we have overlooked the abundant nature of "kairos."

If all we figure out how to is later time (for example, what's next on the schedule), we surrender the "kairos" characteristics of time that make driving best, being entirely present for the open doors right now. Numerous things are deserving within recent memory that in our "time-starved" point of view, we believe we can never cut out time for. A different perspective to investigate is to "cut in" to our current time the characteristics of being that assist us with being progressively viable. Here are a few aspects of managing rather than time.

Here Are 10 Time Management Questions to Ask Yourself Today:

1. What Am I Going to Do Today? – Have you arranged your day? Do you know where you are going before you go out? Take a couple of moments to survey your schedule and arrangements. Knowing where you are going (and when) avoids bunches of emergencies not far

off.

2. What Do I Need to Do Today? – Are you carrying out whatever responsibility comes to your direction first? Or on the other hand, do you have a perspective on your organized errands, with the goal that you can do what is generally significant? Audit your lineup for the day before bouncing into your work.

3. Am I Ready For My Day? – Knowing what you have to do is great; being set up for it is far and away superior. Ensure you have gotten your work done. A couple of moments of preparation before that gathering or errand can have a significant effect.

4. What Are My Long Term Goals? – Do you have long haul objectives? It is safe to say that they are recorded? If you don't, at that point, you are mostly going where life is taking you. Instead, settle on a decision and make your way.

5. What Am I Not Going to Get Done? – There is something that you have to do today that won't complete. You will overlook, or you won't have the opportunity. Pause for a minute to recognize that significant

assignment, regardless of how little it is. It could be to make a regular checkup or to get something in transit home. Make an opportunity to do it.

6. What Did I Promise Someone Else I Would Do Today? – We frequently advise others we will achieve something. And afterward, we don't. Or, on the other hand, we overlook. Do you make guarantees that you don't keep? What do you have to do today for somebody?

7. What Will I Do To Take Care of Myself Today? – You can't generally run at 100%. You need to deal with yourself. Ensure you invest some energy in yourself, regardless of whether it is to practice or make a couple of moments for your hobby.

8. Who Do I Need to Spend Some Time With Today? Too regularly, we get so enveloped with our tasks or our busy schedules that we ignore the individuals that we have to give attention to. Is it a colleague that requirements help? Or then again a relative that needs somebody on-one time?

9. What Did I Do Today? – At the day's end, pause for a minute to audit what you achieved. Keeping a diary

is an extraordinary method to do this. It just feels better, and it lets you survey your advancement. It additionally gives a remarkable life record to yourself or others to pursue sometime in the not so distant future.

10. Am I Happy With What I Did Today? – After you have looked into what you did today, ask yourself, "Am I content with that?" Are you doing what you need to do throughout everyday life? Some of the time we are so bustling making a cursory effort, that we don't understand that we have a decision. It's up to you what you do with your life every day. Pick carefully.

The most famous ancient Greek Philosopher ever, Socrates, was a master stonemason and social critic. He never wrote anything, and the majority of his philosophical commitments get through his understudies, basically Plato. Socrates set out an entirely different point of view of achieving functional outcomes through the utilization of theory in our everyday lives. Socrates got well known for urging individuals to address everything. Socrates' most prominent commitment to philosophy was the Socratic Method, where discourse, contention, and exchange are utilized to observe the reality. In the long run, his beliefs and reasonable methodology, in theory, lead his end, as he was attempted and indicted for criticizing religion and ruining the young. Socrates, at that point, picked death by suicide over outcast from his country of Athens. His legendary trial and death at the raised area of the old Greek majority rule framework have changed the scholarly perspective on theory as an investigation of life itself.

Socrates, the ancient Greek Philosopher, used to give open talks about certain subjects like Life and the afterlife while remaining on a major stone toward the edge of the market. People groups in the market and the passersby come and tune in for a couple of moments and leave when they listen to his way of thinking. They never gave a lot of consideration to his way of thinking. Socrates, when he found that the individuals are not giving a lot of concern regarding his way of thinking, chose to accomplish something else.

Stoicism isn't only some old way of thinking. Its focal thoughts proceeded to motivate the absolute most potent psychological tools of the advanced time, like Cognitive Behavioral Therapy.

And, what was one of those enormous thoughts? Beliefs underlie feelings.

If I point something at you and you trust it's a firearm, you're terrified. If you believe it's a toy weapon, you're most certainly not. You're not mystic or omniscient. It's your beliefs that make your sentiments, not reality.

Don't deal with your state of mind by hesitating. Ask yourself what beliefs underlie your emotions and question those.

Is it true that you fear the assignment? Why? Does it have a blade pointed at you? No. You're afraid you'll do a lousy job. You're going to do a much more dreadful activity if you don't begin.

Change your beliefs, and you change your sentiments. Change your emotions, and you'll achieve more.

Monochronicity, then again, described individuals with a significantly more direct, clock-and schedule-driven way to deal with time. See the area on Time in Different Cultures for more discussion of polychronic and monochronic. The entire investigation of chronemics (the study of how time is seen and esteemed in people and societies, especially as respects non-verbal correspondence). Synchronicity is a related idea, first depicted by the Swiss therapist Carl Jung during the 1920s, where individual encounters at least two occasions as definitively related here and there, even though they are probably not going to be causally related.

CHAPTER 2
THE VALUE OF TIME

Most people look at their financial balances with extraordinary consideration and survey how a lot of cash they need to spend, to contribute, and to part with. However, they don't take a look at their time similarly and wind up squandering this fantastically significant resource. Time is considerably more critical than cash since you can utilize your opportunity to profit. However, you can't use the money to buy additional time.

Time is an incredible equalizer. Every day has just 24 hours; no one has anything else than any other person. Everybody, from writers to presidents, fills those hours in a steady progression until they are altogether topped off. Every moment is remarkable, and once gone, can never be regained.

At the point when you take a look at somebody who has achieved a great deal, you can be almost sure that the individual has invested extensive measures of energy acing the necessary abilities, filling a long time with challenging work. There are the individuals who take a look at others' achievements and state, "I had that thought," or "I could have done that." But thoughts are cheap, and intentions are just that. If you don't contribute the time expected to accomplish those objectives, at that point, the total of what you have is unfulfilled desire.

You can generally figure out how to get more cashflow. Even though it's not something we need to do, we have the choice to sell possessions, work an additional move, get some independent work, or perhaps win a couple of bucks on a scratch ticket. In any case, there are no odds for you to take additional time. You can't add an hour to the day. You can't give yourself 20 additional years on this planet by putting resources into the "time showcase." Time is limited for us, as people. We may have 85 years to live and thrive, or we may get 30. This is worth remembering when you are investing more energy profiting than you are with loved ones. Those occasions are valuable and temporary. Cash?

Most of the humans, Paulinus, complain bitterly of the resentment of Nature, since we are conceived for a short range of life because even this space has been allowed to us surges by so rapidly that all spare a not very many discover life at an end exactly when they are preparing to live.

Nor is it merely the regular group and the careless group that weeps over what is, as men regard it, a universal sick; a similar inclination has called forward objection additionally from well-known men.

It isn't that we have a short space of time, yet that we squander quite a bit of it. Life is sufficiently long, and it has been given in enough liberal measures to allow the achievement of the best things if it's entire is very much contributed. In any case, when it is squandered in luxury and carelessness when it is dedicated to nothing more than a bad memory end, constrained finally by a definitive need, we see that it had died before we knew that it was passing. So it is the existence we get isn't short, yet we make it along these lines, nor do we have any absence of it, yet are inefficient of it. Similarly, as extraordinary and princely wealth is scattered in a minute when it comes under the control of a terrible proprietor, while riches anyway restricted if it is entrusted to a good guardian, increments by use, so our life is sufficiently long for him who orders it appropriately.

"You aren't bothered, would you say you are because you gauge a specific sum and not twice to such an extent? So why get stirred up that you've been given a specific life expectancy and not more? Similarly, as you are happy with your normal weight, so you ought to be with the time you've been given." — Marcus Aurelius, Meditations, 6.49

The state age is only a number, however to specific individuals, it's a significant one something else, ladies wouldn't lie about being more youthful, and aggressive youngsters wouldn't lie about being more seasoned. Wealthy individuals and health nuts burn through billions of dollars with an end goal to move the termination date from around seventy-eight years to hopefully forever.

The number of years we figure out how to squeeze out doesn't make a difference, just what those years are made out of. Seneca put it best when he stated, "Life is long if you realize how to utilize it." Sadly, a great many people don't; they waste the existence they've been given. When it is past the point of no return, do they attempt to make up for that burn through by vainly hoping to put additional time on the clock?

"You fear to pass on. Be that as it may, come currently, how is this life of yours anything besides passing?" — Seneca, Moral Letters, 77.18

Seneca recounts a remarkable story about an obscenely wealthy Roman who was carried around by slaves on a litter. On one event, in the wake of being lifted out of a shower, the Roman asked, "Am I sitting down yet?"

Seneca's point was basically: What sort of tragic wretched life is it in case you're so disconnected from the world that you don't realize whether you're on the ground? How did the man know whether he was even alive by any means?

The more significant part of us afraid of dying. But, here and there, this dread asks the question: To secure what precisely? For many individuals, the appropriate response is long periods of TV, tattling, gorging, wasting potential, reporting to a tedious job, without any end in sight, and on. But, in the strictest sense, is this an actual existence? Is this value grasping so firmly and fearing to lose?

"It's not in the slightest degree that we have too short an opportunity to live, however, that we waste a lot of it. Life is sufficiently long, and it's given inadequate measures to do numerous incredible things if we spend it well. However, when it's poured down the channel of extravagance and disregard when it's utilized to a whole lot of nothing end, we're at last headed to see that it had passed by before we even remembered it passing. Thus it is, we don't get a short life, and we make it so." — Seneca, On the Brevity of Life, 1.3–4a

Nobody realizes to what extent they need to live, yet tragically, we can make sure of a specific something: we'll squander to an extreme degree a lot of life. Waste it sitting around, waste it chasing pursuing inappropriate things, burn through it by declining to require some investment to ask ourselves what's essential to us. Excessively regularly, we're similar to the overconfident academics that Petrarch reprimanded in his excellent article on obliviousness. The sorts who "waste their forces ceaselessly in thinking about things outside of them and look for themselves there." Yet they have no clue this is what they're doing.

So today, if you end upsurged or articulating the words, "I simply need more time," stop and take a second. Is this, in reality, obvious? Or then again, have you quite recently dedicated to a lot of pointless things? It is safe to say that you are being productive, or have you expected a lot of waste into your life? The average American goes through something like forty hours every year in rush hour gridlock. That is a long time through the span of real existence. Furthermore, for "traffic," you can substitute such a significant number of exercises, from battling with others to watching television to daydreaming.

However, there is no purpose behind you to assume that these individuals don't have any idea how valuable a thing time is; for those whom they love most devotedly, they have a habit of saying that they are prepared to give them their very own piece years. And, they do give it, without acknowledging it; however, the consequence of their giving is that they suffer loss without adding to the long periods of their darlings. However, the very thing they don't know is whether they are experiencing loss;

hence, the evacuation of something that is lost, in secret they find, is bearable. However nobody will bring back the years, nobody will offer you again on yourself. Life will follow the way it began upon, and will neither turn around nor check its course; it will make no clamor, it won't help you to remember its quickness. Quiet it will float on; it won't drag out itself at the order of a ruler, or the commendation of the masses.

Similarly, as it was begun its first day, so it will run; no place will it turn aside, no site will it delay.

What's more, what will be the outcome? You have been engrossed; life rushes by; in the meantime, death will be within reach, for which, helter-skelter, you should discover a recreation. Would anything be able to be sillier than the perspective of specific individuals, I mean the individuals who celebrate their foresight? They keep themselves busily occupied with a request that they might have the option to live better; they consume this existence in preparing to live! They structure their motivations with a view to the far off future, yet postponement is the most significant waste of life; it denies them of every day as it comes; it grabs from them the present by promising something hereafter. The best obstruction to living is hope, which relies on the morrow and wastes today. You discard what lies in the hands of Fortune, you let go what lies in your own. Whither do you look? At what objective do you point? Everything that is still to lie in vulnerability lives straightway! Perceive how the best of bards shouts out, and, as though motivated with divine expression, sings the saving strain:

Life is partitioned into three periods, what has been, what is, what will be. Of these the here and now is short, what's to come is short, the past is sure. For the latter is the one over which Fortune has lost control, is the one who can't be brought back under any labor. Be that as it may, men who are engrossed lose this, for they have no opportunity to think again upon the past, and regardless of whether they ought to have, it isn't enjoyable to review something they should see with regret. They are, like this, unwilling to coordinate their contemplations in reverse to not well gone through hours, and those whose vices become evident if they survey the past, even the vices which were masked under some allurement of flashing delight, don't have the mental courage to return to those hours. Nobody readily turns his idea back to the past, except if every one of his demonstrations have been submitted to the oversight of his still, small voice, which is never deceived; he who has ambitiously coveted, proudly scorned, recklessly conquered, treacherously betrayed, greedily seized, or lavishly squandered, must need fear his memory. But then this is the piece within recent memory that is consecrated and set apart, put past the compass of every single human disaster, and expelled from the area of Fortune, the part which is disturbed by no need, by no fear, by no attacks of disease; this can now be grieved nor be grabbed away, it is an everlasting and unanxious ownership. The present offers just a single day at once, and each by minutes; yet every one of the times of past time will show up when you offer them, they will endure you to view them and keep them at your will, a thing which the individuals who are engaged have no opportunity to do. The mind that is untroubled and tranquil can roam into every one of an incredible piece; however, the brains of the fascinated, similarly as though weighted by a burden, can't turn and look behind. Thus their life disappears into a void; and as it does a whole lot of nothing, regardless of how much water you fill a vessel, if there is no base to get and hold it, so with time, it has no effect what amount is given; if there is nothing for it to settle upon, it drops through the chinks and gaps of the brain. Present time is exceptionally brief, so short, for sure, that to some there is by all accounts none; for it is consistently moving, it ever streams and hurries on; it stops to be before it has come, and can no more creek delay than the atmosphere or the stars, whose regularly unresting development never lets them live in a similar track. The fascinated, along these lines, are worried about the present time alone, and it is brief to the point that it can't be gotten a handle on, and even this is filched away from them, diverted as they are among numerous things.

In a word, would you like to know how they don't "live long"? Perceive that they are so anxious to live long! Decrepit older men beg in their prayers for the expansion of a couple of more years; they imagine that they are more youthful than they will be; they comfort themselves with a falsehood, and are as satisfied to mislead themselves as though they tricked Fate simultaneously. In any case, when finally some sickness has helped them to remember their mortality, in what fear do they bite the dust, feeling that they are being hauled out of life, and not just leaving it. They shout out that they have been fools since they have not so much lived, and that they will live hereafter in recreation if only they escape from this sickness; at that point finally, they reflect how pointlessly they have made progress toward things which they didn't appreciate, and how the entirety of their work has gone to no end.

But, for those whose life is passed remote from all business, for what reason would it be advisable for it not to be plentiful? None of it is assigned to another, none of it is dispersed toward this path and that, none of it is focused on Fortune, none of it perishes from neglect, none is subtracted by inefficient giving, none of it is unused; its entire yields salary. Thus, anyway, little it's the measure, it is richly adequate, and along these lines, at whatever point his last day will come, the intelligent man won't stop for a second to go to meet death with steady step.

Yet, the individuals who overlook the past, disregard the present, and dread for the future have a real existence that is exceptionally brief and troubled; when they have arrived at its finish, the miserable frauds see past the point of no return that for such an extended period they have been busied in sitting idle. Nor because they now and again conjure passing, have you any motivation to think it any verification that they discover deep-rooted. In their indiscretion, they are bugged by moving feelings that surge them into the very things they fear; they frequently appeal to God for death since they fear it. And, as well, you have no motivation to imagine this is any verification that they are carrying on quite a while the way that the day regularly appears to them long, the idea that they whine that the hours take a break set for dinner arrives; for, whenever their distractions fail them, they are eager since they are left with nothing to do, and they don't have the foggiest idea how to discard their relaxation or to haul out the time. Thus they take a stab at another thing to possess them, and all the mediating time is annoying; precisely as they do when a gladiatorial display is declared, or when they are sitting tight for the delegated time of some other show or delight, they need to skirt the days that lie between. All postponement of something they trust appears to belong to them. However, the time which they appreciate is short and quick, and it is made a lot shorter by their very own flaw, for they escape starting with one joy then onto the next and can't stay fixed in one want. Thus, my dearest Paulinus, tear yourself away from the group, and, an excessive amount of storm-tossed for the time you have lived, finally pull back into a peaceful harbor. Consider what number of waves you have experienced, what number of storms, from one perspective, you have continued in private life, what number of, on the other, you have brought upon yourself in open life; long enough has your virtue been shown in laborious and constant confirmations, attempt how it will carry on in relaxation. Most of your life, absolutely its better piece, has been given to the state; take now some portion of your time for yourself also. Also, I don't gather you to slothful or idle inaction, or to suffocate all your local vitality in sleep and the delights that are of high repute to the group. That isn't to rest; you will discover far more noteworthy works than every one of those you have up to this point performed so energetically, to possess you amidst your discharge and retirement. You, I know, deal with the records of the entire world as sincerely as you would a stranger's, as cautiously as you would your own, as conscientiously as you would the states. You win love in an office in which it is hard to stay away from scorn, yet by and by trusting me, it is smarter to know about the record of one's own life than of the corn-market.

Need to begin esteeming your time somewhat more since you trust it will make you more joyful? Whillans recommend changing how you go through your cash. Work less additional time hours, spring the extra $20 for a taxi home if the transport is going to take longer or go to the pricier market that is nearer to your home, so you possess more energy for things you appreciate.

"The key is making sure that in addition to using money to have additional time, individuals also invest their free energy in better manners," Whillans says, including that "better ways" would incorporate dedicating time to things that fulfill you. For a few of us, that means relaxing on a seashore, while others need to invest energy with loved ones. My theory is that you can take additional time, yet if the thing you do with it doesn't make you content, you most likely won't be happier when all is said in done. Monitoring what makes us truly glad is also an unquestionable requirement so that you can put that opportunity to great use.

CHAPTER 3
THE PHILOSOPHY OF TIME MANAGEMENT TODAY

Here is the irony recorded as a hard copy of a piece about the interruption. I let myself know not to browse my email until the segment was done, yet I peaked at my Facebook because I was awaiting a reaction. I saw that I had four new friend requests, so during the time spent accepting them, I see that another blogger has referenced one of my posts in an ongoing site, so I click over to her website.

Goodness, and did I notice that I have Mozart shooting endlessly in my ears with the goal that I can overwhelm the sound of the web recording the lady before me at the café is playing?

I have realized continuously that distraction is an issue for me. At the point when I was lesser in secondary school, I was taken to a therapist to be assessed. He told my mom that my decoding skills (capacity to decipher, decrypt, solve, translate)) were the absolute poorest he'd seen. In this way, to give myself the absolute best at focus, I'd carry around wax ear fittings and push those things highly into my ear waterways, to shut out the tapping of a pencil alongside me or the sigh of the person three work areas away. To keep myself concentrated on the paper before me, I'd imagine a lot of blinders for my eyes and an imaginary fortress around my work area.

However, as per Maggie Jackson, journalist for the Boston Globe and writer of the book "Occupied: The Erosion of Attention and the Coming Dark Age," there is substantially more in question in our way of life today in light of innovation than a couple of bad test scores and an endemic of decoding issues. Maggie says, "How we live is dissolving our ability for deep, continued perceptive consideration the structure square of closeness, wisdom, and social advancement. Additionally, this crumbling may come at an extraordinary expense to ourselves and society. The erosion of consideration is the way to understanding why we are on the cusp of a period of across the board social and social losses."

Maggie didn't decide to compose a book about

interruption and the job of attention regarding a culture. She was curious regarding why such a large number of individuals are worried and feel caught in compelled lives in spite of the considerable number of resources we have as a nation. In her exploration, she found that in spite of the significant amount of points of interest of our mechanical tools, they are achieving similar issues innate in the principal modern and high-tech (telegraph, cinema, and railway) revolutions. Moreover, she was shocked to learn in her exploration how focal consideration is to a culture, and what happens when you let go of the powers of attention.

Concerning me, this piece took an extra hour to write because I couldn't avoid checking my email, just as following up on my tweets on Twitter and reading my Facebook and LinkedIn mail. I presume I am a decent a valid example for Maggie's examination. But, all expectation isn't lost. Says Maggie: "We can make a culture of consideration, recoup the capacity to stop, center, interface, judge, and enter deep into a relationship or a thought." We do that consideration activities and utilizing something I have a lack of recently, discipline.

Or on the other hand, Maggie says, "we can slip into numb long stretches of simple diffusion and detachment.... The choice is ours."

Recollect your objectives from a minute prior. Presently attempt to imagine what your technologies' goals are for you. What do you think they are? I don't mean the organizations' statements of purpose and high-flying advertising messages. I mean the objectives on the dashboards in their item design meetings, the measurements they're utilizing to coordinate your consideration, to characterize what achievement implies for your life. How likely is it that they mirror the objectives you have for yourself?

Not likely, sadly. From their point of view, the achievement is quite often characterized as low-level "engagement" goals, as they're frequently called. These incorporate things like expanding the measure of time you go through with their item, keeping you clicking or tapping or looking however much as could be expected, or demonstrating you the same number of pages or promotions as they can. Be that as it may, these "engagement" goals are negligible, subhuman objectives.

No individual has these objectives for themselves. Nobody gets up toward the beginning of the day and asks: "How much time can I spend utilizing online life today?" (If there is somebody like that, I'd love to meet them and understand their brain.)

What this means is that there's a profound misalignment between the objectives we set for ourselves and the purposes that a significant number of data innovations have for us. This appears to me to be a considerable arrangement and one that nobody discusses enough. We confide in these technologies to befriend frameworks for our lives: we believe them to assist us with doing the things we need to do, to turn into the individuals we need to be. We trust them to be our side.

If you needed to prepare all of society to be as rash and feeble willed as could be allowed, how might you do it? One way is to design an impulsivity preparing gadget – we should consider it an iTrainer – that conveys a perpetual stock of instructive awards on request. You'd need to make it sufficiently little to fit in a pocket or tote so individuals could convey it anyplace they went. The educational prizes it would pipe into their attentional world could be anything, from adorable feline photographs to tidbits of news that shock you (since shock can, all things considered, be a prize as well). To help its viability, you could supply the iTrainer with productive frameworks of insight and robotization so it could adjust to clients' practices, settings, and individual characteristics to get them to invest however much energy and consideration with it as could reasonably be expected.

So suppose you construct the iTrainer and circulate it continuously into society. From the start, individuals' resolution would likely be entirely reliable and safe. The iTrainer may likewise cause cumbersome social circumstances, at least until enough individuals had received it with the goal that it was broadly acknowledged. Be that as it may, if everybody somehow managed to continue utilizing it more than quite a while, you'd most likely begin seeing it work genuinely well. Presently, the iTrainer may make individuals' lives harder to live: it would no uncertainty impede the successful quest for their ideal errands and objectives. Even though you made it, you most likely wouldn't let your children utilize one. However, from the perspective of your plan objectives, i.e., making the world progressively indiscreet and feeble willed, it would most likely be a thundering achievement.

At that point, imagine a scenario in which you needed to take things considerably further. Imagine a situation where you needed to make everybody much increasingly diverted, angry, skeptical – and even uncertain of what, or how, to think. Consider the possibility that you needed to troll everybody's psyches. You'd presumably make an engine, a lot of financial impetuses, which would make it beneficial for others to create and convey these prizes – and, where conceivable, you'd make these the primary motivations for doing as such. You don't need only any compensations to get conveyed – you need individuals to get rewards that address their incautious selves, remunerates that are the best at punching the correct fastens in their cerebrums. For good measure, you could likewise incorporate the responsibility for structure; however much as could be expected.

What Is Delayed Gratification?

What do you do at the yearly organization Christmas

party when you experience platters of tasty and enticing foods when you are attempting to get more fit? If you surrender and top off your plate with stuffing treats, it may wreck you're eating regimen, yet you will get the opportunity to appreciate a touch of instant satisfaction.

If you figure out how to oppose and go through the night eating plate of mixed greens and munching on carrot sticks, at that point, you will get a considerably more noteworthy reward down the line—shedding those undesirable pounds and having the option to fit into your preferred pair of thin pants.

This capacity to oppose allurement and adhere to our objectives is frequently alluded to as resolve or discretion, and postponing delight is regularly observed as a focal piece of this behavior. We put off what we need now with the goal that we can maybe get something different, something better, later on.

Picking a long term award over quick gratification represents a significant test in numerous everyday issues. From maintaining a strategic distance from a cut of chocolate cake when we are attempting to get more fit to remaining at home to ponder as opposed to going out to a gathering with companions, the capacity to defer delight can mean the distinction between accomplishing our objectives or not. Do you have the ability to oppose and get a later—and surprisingly better—reward?

Researchers have discovered that this capacity to postpone gratification isn't only a significant piece of objective accomplishment. It may likewise majorly affect long term life achievement and general prosperity.

The Stanford Marshmallow Experiment

In exemplary psychology research from the 1970s, a clinician named Walter Mischel put a treat before kids and offered them a decision—they could either appreciate the gift now or hold up a brief timeframe to get two snacks. At the point when the experimenter left the room, a considerable lot of the children quickly ate the treat (regularly a treat or marshmallow). Yet, a part of the children had the option to put off the inclination to appreciate the gift now and hang tight for the award of getting two heavenly treats later on.

What Mischel found was that the children that had the option to defer gratification had various preferences later on over the children who mostly couldn't pause. The children who had sat tight for the treatment performed preferred scholastically over children that destroyed the treat right. The individuals who postponed their satisfaction additionally showed fewer behavioral issues and later had a lot higher SAT scores.

Why Is It So Hard to Wait?

So if the capacity to control our driving forces and postpone gratification is so significant, how precisely can individuals approach improving this capacity?

In follow-up tests, Mischel found that utilizing various interruption methods helped children defer satisfaction all the more viably. Such systems included singing tunes, pondering something different, or covering their eyes.

Postponing gratification isn't generally so straightforward in reality, however. While the children in Mischel's examination had the guarantee of an auxiliary compensation for standing by only a brief timeframe, regular situations don't generally accompany this assurance. If you surrender that brownie, regardless, you probably won't shed pounds if you avoid a get-together to think about, despite everything you may do ineffectively on the test.

It is this vulnerability that makes surrendering quick rewards so troublesome. That tasty treat before you currently is a slam dunk. However, your objective of shedding pounds appears to be a lot further off and not all that certain.

Neuroscientists Joseph W. Kable and Joseph T. McGuire of the University of Pennsylvania propose that our vulnerability about potential compensations is the thing that makes postponing gratification such a test. "The planning of genuine occasions isn't generally so unsurprising," they clarify. "Chiefs routinely sit tight for transports, employment propositions, weight reduction, and different results described by the critical fleeting vulnerability."

We don't have the foggiest idea when these long term rewards will show up—or whether they will ever show up.

Trust Is a Critical Factor

Whether you are happy to hold up might depend a ton on your perspective. Do you hang tight for something if you aren't sure it will ever truly occur? Do you have confidence in your capacities to get things going or believe that your objectives will happen?

In a later take on Mischel's renowned experiment, cognitive science student Celeste Kidd of the University of Rochester investigated this issue of trust. The test was equivalent to Mischel's, however down the middle of the cases, the analysts broke their guarantee of offering a subsequent treat and instead gave the kids only a conciliatory sentiment.

At the point when they ran the investigation a subsequent time, most of the children who got the guaranteed treat in the main trial were by and by ready to hold up to get a subsequent treatment. The children who had been deceived the first run through around weren't eager to hold up this time—they gobbled the marshmallows after the researchers left the room.

The most effective method to Increase the Ability to

Delay Gratification

- A few techniques that may assist you with improving your capacity to defer gratification include:

- Give final time allotments: In a circumstance where individuals don't know when they will get a reasonable prize, giving feedback on precisely to what extent they should hold up can be helpful. Train stations may post hold up times, for instance, while teachers may provide students with a complete cutoff time for when students will get a guaranteed prize.

- Set realistic deadlines: When attempting to accomplish an objective, for example, getting in shape, individuals are now and again inclined to either setting ridiculous deadlines. For instance, an individual attempting to get in shape will set himself up for disappointment on the off chance that he makes an absurd objective of shedding 10 pounds for each week. At the point when he neglects to lose those initial 10 pounds, he may then surrender and yield to allurement. An increasingly practical objective of one pound for each week would enable him to see the positive consequences of his endeavors.

Advantages of Delayed Gratification

Studies show that delayed gratification is one of the best close to home characteristics of productive individuals. Individuals who figure out how to deal with should be fulfilled at the time flourish more in their vocations, connections, wellbeing, and funds than individuals who surrender to it.

Having the option to defer fulfillment isn't the least demanding expertise to procure. It includes feeling disappointed, which is the reason it appears to be outlandish for individuals who haven't figured out how to control their motivations. Deciding to have something currently may feel better, yet attempting to have taught and deal with your motivations can bring about greater or better prizes later on. After some time, deferring satisfaction will improve your self-control and, at last, assist you with accomplishing your long-term objectives quicker.

A well-known study led at Stanford University during the 1960s clarifies a great deal regarding why it's gainful to postpone gratification. In the examination, kids were set in a stay with one marshmallow on a plate. The lead scientist gave the kids simple guidance: You can eat the marshmallow now, or hold up 15 minutes and get two marshmallows. The scientists found that the kids who had the option to hang tight for the second marshmallow without eating the first scored higher on government-sanctioned tests, would be advised to wellbeing, and were more reluctant to have behavior issues.

Think about the aftereffects of this examination, and consider yourself and your activities. Is it true that you are ready to hang tight for things you truly need, whether it includes yielding joy and fulfillment now? Do you settle on choices dependent on your life reason or on what feels great at this point? Do you, at times, surrender too early? Would you be able to think about when you achieved a troublesome assignment? How could it make you feel about yourself? What were the aftereffects of pausing?

The resilience you display when sitting tight for something you need says a ton regarding you. If there's something you need to purchase, will you spare presently to pay with money later, or pay with a charge card now and pay yourself back later? If you began school or claim your very own business and aren't seeing the rewards yet, will you continue onward or surrender when difficulties arise?

What is your relationship with money? Do you love to spare and spending plans for the future, or would you say you are tied in with getting a charge out of that well-deserved money and arranged to stray into the red for it? In any case, we have to show signs of improvement at discussing it If we ever need to be better at overseeing it, and in the end, having a more significant amount of it. Mainly when you think about that universally, ladies control upwards of $20 trillion in yearly consumer spending. Yet, tragically, with regards to overseeing cash, ladies aren't as autonomous as you'd anticipate. A negligible 11% of millennial ladies in hetero connections confess to assuming responsibility for their monetary future. That implies 91% of women aren't taking part in money related choices. Our new arrangement, The Money Files, is set to change all that by helping women become experts in their accounts so they can deal with their cash and their future.

Money. We, as a whole, love, spending it, and we, as a whole, need a higher amount of it, yet sparing it is the crucial step. It isn't so much that we would prefer not to see more cash in the bank (duh); however, finding some harmony between putting something aside for the future and carrying on with the existence you need isn't always a simple one to master. Time and again, the pendulum swings more distant into the spending camp, and before you know it, you're operating at a profit and playing make up for lost time with the intrigue charged on your credit card debt.

Try not to stress; we get it. That is the reason we asked Priya Malani, an accomplice of Stash Wealth, to help every one of us get our money-related crap together. In this way, she sent us ten significant money questions to pose to ourselves so we can bank that cash, take care of that obligation, and live like a millionaire (well, that is the fantasy).

1. What can I sensibly do to improve my income level?

Negotiation is never a poorly conceived notion as long as you've anticipated it. Most managers plan for you to haggle as there's squirm room in your pay run. A yearly exchange is superbly fitting. Utilize the months driving up the discussion to prime your supervisor and report the evidence that you'll utilize while going in for the ask.

When is a negotiation not shrewd? At the point when you go in cold and request a raise. You'll need to have information to help your solicitation and documentation of your worth include (whether it's subjective, not quantitative). Stay factional and apathetic or, more all, abandon governmental issues.

Side note: IMHO, needing to update your way of life, is not a solid motivation to request a raise. I was as of late addressing somebody who was encouraged to utilize this system, and as an entrepreneur, I can say that not exclusively would it not work. Yet, it would leave me with a more unfortunate assessment of the representative's capacity to #adult. Taking e-courses that are digressively identified with your field is a superb method to show the pledge to expanding efficiency and esteem and bolsters your case for a raise.

2. What would I be able to do to turn around bad credit and recover my score on track?

This may sound strange, however, start utilizing a credit card and taking care of it in full every week or all the more frequently. This is one of my most loved FICO hacks (FICO is a contraction for the Fair Isaac Corporation, the leading organization to offer an acknowledge chance model for a score). It's a speedy and straightforward to way decidedly affect one of the most significant pieces of your financial assessment—your credit utilization ratio. Make a point to never to energize beyond what you can pay off.

If your Mastercards are maxed, discover ways you can settle that obligation ASAP. Consider Airbnb's a room in your home, selling stuff on FB Marketplace or through Poshmark, getting a house, cutting any unnecessary costs that may free up money that you can put towards your obligation. What's more, when you locate the additional money, set up a customary obligation reimbursement automation, so you don't inadvertently spend it.

If you need to investigate different activities that may knock your score, download the CreditWise app (it's free), which incorporates a credit score simulator. It gives you how various actions will affect your credit score before you focus on doing them. I'm an immense fan of this application and use it myself.

3. Am I at a reasonable savings pace for what I need to do when I'm close to retirement age? What amount would it be advisable for me to be putting something aside for retirement?

There's no simple answer here because retirement isn't one-size-fits-all. You can begin by utilizing an online adding machine to discover the amount you'd have to take care of to guarantee you'll supplant a bit your present salary when you hit your ideal retirement age.

Here are the principle things you have to consider:

- How much you procure now?

- Is it only you in retirement, or would you say you are accommodating another person?

- At what age would you like to resign?

- How long do you expect your retirement enduring (otherwise known as future – MORBID, I know!)

When you decide these things, you'll have the significant sources of info that will assist you with choosing the amount you ought to take care of for the precise retirement you picture for yourself. Indeed, it's tough to imagine what your life may resemble a long time from now, yet I have three words for you: Playing. Get up to speed. Sucks.

4. In case I'm anticipating having kids, how might I guarantee I have enough funds to deal with them on one income? What's more, when would it be a good idea for me to begin putting something aside for their schooling?

A good exercise is to bury 10-15% of your income today and perceive how it feels. That is the level of your income that will go towards your children for fundamental everyday costs (excluding schooling). If you believe you can oversee on 85-90% of what comes in the entryway that is a good sign that you have space for kids, monetarily.

With regards to putting something aside for school, everything relies upon how a lot of help you need to give them. 100% of four years at a private establishment? Half of four years at an open establishment? When you know what your needs are here, you'll have the option to once again into your reserve funds objective. Add that reserve funds objective to the 10-15% I talked about before and plan to live without that money—is it possible? Assuming this is the case, start sparing at the earliest opportunity.

Indeed, it's unpleasant to play get up to speed, and the more you pause, the more you'll need to spare to be on track for your objective.

5. What might occur if my spouse passed away? How might I plan for that?

This is a not fun thing to consider and get ready for, yet it's entirely critical to do as such. With regards to the monetary help your life partner gives, the initial step is to choose whether you feel reliant on your companion salary or if you possess property or have children together. Assuming this is the case, extra security may bode well. A life coverage individual can assist you with assessing how much inclusion to acquire to guarantee that if your life partner dies, you wouldn't need to change your way of life, at the end of the day, you'd, in any case, have the option to pay your home loan and deal with your children similarly you are currently (financially).

6. When would it be a good idea for me to begin contributing money? Also, how would I realize what to put resources into?

This question deserves an entire article all by itself. In any case, the bottom line is this. Contributing is a route for your cash to develop after some time, not medium-term. If you think contributing prompts a "fast win," you're contemplating everything incorrectly. Money Street wants to depict providing increasingly like betting, yet the truth is that the sooner you start contributing, the more fruitful you'll be because money develops with time, and you should show restraint for it to work?

To the extent of what to put resources into, this is another zone Wall Street (and the media) depicts inaccurately. They cause it to appear your help to pick stocks and exchange habitually when the inverse, in reality, is valid—unwavering mindsets always win in the end. If you've at any point known about record reserves, you're progressing nicely.

Contributing is a way to achieve your financial goals; thus, in fact, nobody should mention to you what to put resources into until they comprehend what you're contributing for. Goal setting is the initial step to realizing what to put resources into.

7. How might I put something aside for a house? What do I have to do?

Addressing my point over, the initial step to take is to resolve to homeownership as a financial goal. In case you're seeing someone, need to have this discussion with your SO. Characterize the period wherein you'd prefer to achieve purchasing a home. Utilizing destinations like Zillow can enable you to assess what sort of home you'd prefer to buy and the amount it will cost. When you realize what you're focusing on, you can once again into the amount you'll need to put something aside for an upfront installment. About 20% is a generally standard initial installment, yet numerous Millennials are selecting 10% down to get into a home sooner. This is fine as long as you have the income to cover the mortgage with wiggle room. You would prefer not to wind up #house miserable.

8. How might I make spending that still enables me to carry on with the existence I need? Are there any applications that I can utilize?

YNAB is an incredible app that causes you to isolate your cash into various buckets so you can save money for your needs first (lease, charges, student loan payments) and afterward blow the rest, irreproachable. At Stash, we call it Reverse Budgeting.

9. Would it be a good idea for me to have a financial planner? How would I discover one that is directly for me and won't be

excessively expensive?

Financial planners fill some needs, yet their primary occupation is to assist you with thinking about your short, mid and long term financial goals and afterward figure out a course of action that places you on track in the most financially savvy, charge proficient way. A few people feel good making sense of this all alone, while others think they may profit by a guided discussion. A good financial planner can likewise fill in as go-between when you're in a relationship and give that unprejudiced outside supposition that is now and then the precise thing your life partner needs to get notification from another person. A few people feel they've done something right and utilize a financial planner basically for a second assessment from an accomplished proficient.

At last, a financial planner realizes that you may not know every one of the things you ought to consider and makes recommendations to ensure there aren't any gaps in your arrangement. Stash Wealth is a virtual financial planning firm for HENRYs ™ [High Earners, Not Rich Yet] who are in their 20s and 30s and need to take their money related life to the following level. Reserve Wealth is a trustee (no irreconcilable situations) and charges a onetime level expense to fabricate you a modified approach, called the Stash Plan.

10. Do I have enough for an emergency fund? What amount would it be a good idea for me to keep in that fund?

In contrast to a most financial professional, Stash Wealth accepts your Emergency Fund ought to be close to a quarter of a year worth of your fixed costs (lease, bills, and so forth). Most personal financial gurus talk around six to a year. However, we imagine that it is insane for four reasons:

1. Your Emergency Fund should be your first line of defense, not your lone line of defense.

2. Millennials are hawkers. If sh*t hits the fan, we're at once in our vocations where we can reset our earnings before long (obviously, you realize your industry best)

3. We have such a large number of other financial priorities. Holding up until we've set aside a half year in real money makes they burn through valuable time that

could have been exceptionally utilized, helping us accomplish other financial goals.

4. That's an excessive amount of cash sitting in cash. On a par with the online banks are (and that is the place we'd suggest you keep your Emergency Fund), your money is as yet losing worth consistently on account of expansion. Twenty to thirty-year-olds need their money working harder for them.

CHAPTER 4
HAVE YOUR GOALS WRITTEN

We know the significance of goal setting. However, on most occasions, our goals are not measurable and characterized. You hear individuals make statements like "I need to get thinner," however, losing weight is a goal. It tends to be described if you include things like: "I need to get in shape by eating well and working out. At the point when you analyze both statements, the first just states what you plan to do, the subsequent one states what you mean to do and how you expect to do it.

According to a study on goal setting, individuals who record their goals are bound to achieve it than the individuals who don't. A group of students was going to graduate, and they were approached to set goals for themselves. Some didn't set goals, and some managed without keeping in touch with them down. However, a little late in the gathering wrote down their goals. After numerous years this equivalent group of students was met, and some extremely astonishing was found. The individuals who set objectives and never kept in touch with them were earning twice as much as the individuals who never set any intentions, and the individuals who set goals and thought of them down were winning tenfold the amount of as the individuals who set goals yet never thought of them down.

The vast majority try not to record their goals; instead, they float through life, asking why their arrangements never work out, and this is because of the way that they don't understand the significance of recorded goals.

The secret of achieving your goals in life includes keeping in touch with them down in a well-characterized and transparent way. In this article, I will be taking a look at the significance of recording unmistakably characterized goals.

The significance of recording goals
1. Serves as a reminder

Recording your goals helps you to remember what you are attempting to accomplish. Bright enough we overlook such a large number of smart thoughts without acknowledging it, they vanish when they spring up in our brains. One approach to help hold this under tight restraints is to record your thoughts when they fly into your mind. At the point when you see the goals you have recorded, you are helped to remember your goal. At the point when we have something helping us to remember what we intend to accomplish, there is each probability of doing that thing.

2. It's a method for bringing your vision into the real world

Our thoughts will stay stuck in our minds until we record them and focus on achieving them. A great many people have grand dreams for their lives, however not until it is recorded, the danger of not achieving their goals.

3. It very well may be utilized as a method of tracking your progress

During the time spent executing your goals is essential to monitor progress made along the line. You ought to also f+monitor your failures; that way, you are likely not to rehash the slip-ups that caused you to come up short. At the point when you have a record of the advancement made during the time spent achieving your goals, you will feel urged to invest more energy.

It will also assist you in knowing what's working that you should embrace and what's not working that you should drop.

4. It causes you to filter opportunities

As you make progress in specific parts of your life, you will discover more open doors coming in your direction. In some cases, these open doors become an interruption that can push you off track. So to take care of this issue, you should evaluate your list of written down goals consistently and set aside those things that may push you off course.

Everyone defines goals. A few of us are extraordinarily formal with this procedure, recording our goals, and setting updates for their proposed consummation. Others are significantly more relaxed, almost flippant, relegating their goals to absolutely mental contemplations like "I should deal with that sometime in the future," or "I want to be _____."

Regardless of how you approach your goal setting procedure or how genuinely you take your goals, it's sensible to expect that if you get a more exceptional level of your goals, you'd be more joyful. You may be further along in your vocation, more beneficial in your day by day life, or progressively occupied with your connections. The points of interest don't make a difference; what is essential is that you set goals since you need something, and very regularly, you miss the mark regarding those goals.

So, at that point, how might you make your goals progressively feasible? It is conceivable, and you can do this for practically any goal in as meager as five stages.

Stage One: Make Sure Your Expectations Are Reasonable

The initial step is to ensure your goal is achievable from an intelligent point of view, that is. It's anything but challenging to capitulate to optimistic guesses for goals, for example, needing to turn into a tycoon in a year or learn five new languages in the following three years.

Oppose this temptation. Begin with the primary point of convergence of your goal. For instance, is your objective to turn into a millionaire mogul or to be in an ideal situation? Knowledge will assist you with narrowing your goal in a progressively sensible arrangement, for example, "turning into a millionaire in ten years" or "saving $50,000 in one year."

For this progression, it's a smart thought to do some exploration. Look into data about your goal and converse with individuals who have achieved it. How far have they gone? To what extent did it take them? What assets did they have? Before the finish of this progression, you ought to have a goal that is, in fact, achievable dependent on the assets and capacities you have at present.

Stage Two: Break Your Goal Down Into Smaller Goals

Now that you have a "center" objective set up, you can begin separating it into littler goals. Many people give up on goals that appear to be excessively inaccessible, excessively unpredictable, or just overly scary, so as opposed to facing one huge goal, make yourself meet a few small goals, each in turn. For instance, if you will probably shed 20 pounds, you can set up separate goals of practicing day by day, eliminating with a large portion of the low-quality food from your eating routine, and eating more leafy foods. If you likely land a specific vocation, you can set up discrete goals of accomplishing a confirmation, creating an experience through random temp jobs and shadowing. Systems administration to manufacture your industry contact list. As you would envision, these "littler" goals can be separated much further.

Stage Three: Establish a Timeline for Those Goals

Every one of your small goals ought to have a course of events connected to it. You may end up taking a shot at various little goals simultaneously or taking them out, consistently, in an immediate arrangement. Whichever way is fine, try to guarantee you remain on track to achieve your "center" goal by keeping your smaller goals on a time allotment. For instance, if your fundamental goal is to get familiar with another language, allow yourself a month to become familiar with the nuts and bolts, two extra months to repeat individually, and afterward two additional months to begin repeating with a local speaker (on the web or face to face), trailed by an trip to a nation that speaks your chosen language.

Stage Four: Hold Yourself Accountable

At this point, you ought to have a proper arrangement for how you'll achieve your goal with time-explicit, significant steps to keep you in a sensible, direct way. In any case, how are you going to guarantee you complete those means? You need to figure out how to make yourself responsible for those goals. A primary method to do this is to educate every one of your companions and family members concerning your goals; this will cause them to catch up with you, and inspire you if you ever want to stop. You can also build a progression of series or potentially disciplines to help manage you along. For instance, you may permit yourself a little spending spree when you hit a specific achievement or give yourself less spare time if you haven't accomplished something by a particular date.

Stage Five: Stay Inspired

You were motivated, at the point when you made your unique goal. A quarter of a year into achieving it, it's anything but difficult to lose that initial gut feeling. Make it a point to keep yourself inspired any way you see fit. It very well may be something straightforward like an "inspiration playlist" of melodies that move you, or something progressively included like hiring a fitness coach or having customary sessions with a guide to prop you up. Test to see which strategies work best to motivate you and stick with what works. With these five stages, practically any objective can get feasible. Presently, regardless of whether you achieve it or not is completely up to you. With a sensible desire, a bit by bit strategy, a course of events, a source of inspiration, and some degree of individual responsibility, all that remaining parts is establishing the pieces. Make certain to reward yourself at whatever point you arrive at a new

At the repoint, when you set a significant goal, you're genuinely doling out yourself a large number of little tasks. At the point when individuals abandon these huge goals, it's frequently because they haven't explained what those a great many small assignments are or made arrangements for the time and work required.

I was helped to remember this when tuning in to an ongoing scene of "Another Mother Runner" web recording. Running Coach MK Fleming shared that she urges her customers to concentrate on attainable goals versus huge, radical-sounding achievements. "We become involved with the sort and the conceivable outcomes and set huge goals. Before the finish of January, a great many people have surrendered [on their New Year's resolutions] because they didn't imagine what was extremely important to achieve that goal."

Nobody needs to work you out of a big goal I included. You should seek what you need most throughout everyday life. However, you ought to be sensible about where you are today, where you need to go and what you can sensibly achieve in the period and with the assets you've allocated. If, upon reflection, you don't generally have the opportunity or information required to get where you need to go, it bodes well to set an increasingly achievable goal.

When you meet that first goal, you guarantee yourself

to set one more and again. The gradual methodology is increasingly viable because it ensures probably some advancement towards your big, ultimate goal. It doesn't need to be "all or nothing" circumstance.

How can you tell if a goal is too big?

In some cases, we don't realize enough to realize when we've bitten off something over the top. This is the point at which a mentor or a learned, believed companion could help. The question you ask them isn't, "Is this big goal workable for me?" The question is, "What is the most legitimate initial step I should take?

Here is the measure of energy, and possibly, and potentially cash I'm willing and ready to submit." You don't need to take their recommendations. However, it should be a thought.

When you've defined a goal, you have to make achieving that goal piece of your day by day life. Any goal you take a shot without a moment's delay a week or once a month is bound to be overlooked or pushed down on your need list. To battle this, another "habit stack" is required. A habit stack is a progression of little activities you do in moderately a similar request every day. A large portion of us has a habit stack when preparing for bed that incorporates washing your face, brushing your teeth, and setting your caution, for example. You never (or once in a while) avoid a stage because the habit is established, and you go starting with one action then the next without even thinking about it. We can utilize patterns to further our potential benefit when defining goals. For instance, if you need to run a 10K this year, you'll have to run each day (or consistently) to practice, so set out your running garments and confirm your mileage the previous night.

This is only one case of a little change in your day by day life planned for helping you achieve a bigger goal. Goals that are "correct measured" comparative with the measure of time and work you're willing and ready to contribute are considerably more fulfilling because, mostly, you're bound to achieve them. Achieving a goal is a gigantically motivating experience and one that will construct certain that you can work planning something remarkable after some time. As you set objectives this year, defeat the "all or nothing" outlook and appreciate more achievement in the long-term.

When You Should Set Goals

Each January, a massive number of new goal-setting posts are typically discharged over the web. I state "typically" because the beginning of a New Year is an emblematically incredible update that you should look to better yourself.

There's only one issue: it's arbitrary.

I will wager that goals set on January first are measurably bound to come up short than goals set on some other day of the year. That is because those goals are filled by a temporary enthusiasm, as opposed to a profound situated want.

I, as of late discovered a picture shared by a companion on Facebook that superbly encapsulated this:

There is anything but a single individual on the planet who hasn't had a minute like the above at any rate once in their life. Motivating yourself to achieve tough goals is intense. But then, with regards to figuring out how to set goals, the above approach exemplifies all that you shouldn't do.

My point is this: an objective that merits setting merits fixing now. Not next Monday. Not in the New Year. Today. If you end up delaying, that is because the goal isn't that important to you.

The Logical Thought Process behind Any Goal

Following directly on from that announcement, I should make something completely clear: since you don't see a goal to be significant enough at some random minute doesn't imply that is anything but a goal worth seeking after.

We should not be characterized by our weakest minutes; we should look to our snapshots of most noteworthy solidarity to distinguish what we do with our life. Furthermore, to make sense of whether a goal merits focusing on, we should attempt to analyze whether it justifies the effort objectively.

At the point when I was a child, I skied into a French couple at extraordinary speed (unintentionally). Everything I could state was, "Je Suis très desolate!"

Let's consider two simple examples:

1. I can't communicate in French. The explanation behind this is because there is no genuine advantage to me knowing the language, past the delight of just remembering it. While I might want to communicate in French smoothly, the time and effort venture, it would cost is only not justified, despite any potential benefits to me.

2. I can utilize the WordPress blogging stage. I hadn't known about it 15 months prior, and now I get paid to compose for WordPress-related websites. This blog is based on the WordPress stage. It was certainly worth my time and exertion venture to figure out how to utilize WordPress.

If I had invested as a lot of energy in the course of recent months learning French as I had found out about WordPress, I dare to figure that I would have the option to talk proficiently with local speakers. The explanation that I am a capable WordPress client, yet I can't speak more than around 50 expressions of French, is because learning WordPress offered me more.

This logic applies to anything you need to accomplish in your life. The question you should pose to yourself is: "Will the important effort I need to place in to achieve this goal be coordinated or surpassed by the advantageous result?" If the appropriate response is accurate, you've quite recently shaped the hold of inspiration that you should depend upon to achieve this goal.

Knowing When a Goal is worth it

If the above question were anything but difficult to reply (and enough to keep us propelled over the long-term), we would all be overachievers. In any case, we're not, so different components are affecting everything.

That carries me to an email I sent to my supporters two or three weeks back in which I said the following:

More often than not, our brain makes a tolerable showing of performing intuitive mental gymnastics and giving us the imperative degree of self-discipline identifying with a specific assignment (which might be the required amount).

I utilize the words "more often than not" purposely,

because there is a crucial factor that can slant our interior self-discipline number cruncher (as I have quite recently instituted it): ignorance.

The most significant advance to achieving a goal is in understanding the fundamental endeavor and valuing the potential result. These are not complete terms, except if your objective is basic, you won't completely appreciate those two elements. However, the closer you are to understanding the necessary undertaking and potential result, the better you will have the option to motivate yourself.

So with regards to defining objectives, you should be as instructed as conceivable on what you set out to achieve. Look to enable yourself with information. As

I said in the email to my supporters:

Challenge your brain's logic. Jab gaps in it. Argue for the sake of arguing. Instruct yourself better. Accept guidance from the individuals who have just achieved what you wish for.

The more you think about what you need to achieve, the better prepared you will be to make it.

How to Set Goals: The Big Picture

As I would like to think, there ought to be no depiction of "individual" and "business" goals. I don't care for utilizing those words in such a unique situation since it goes totally against the Leaving Work Behind way of thinking.

At last, you need to better yourself. Regardless of whether that is getting better at baseball or procuring a six-figure pay, the entirety of your goals should remain under a similar umbrella. Your life goals shouldn't be sectioned.

That is the reason I allude to "the comprehensive view" purposely. The initial step you should take in defining goals is to bring a top-down perspective on what you need, given what I consider to be the fundamental classifications that characterize us as people:

1. Happiness
2. Health
3. Success
4. Wealth

5. Giving

6. Growth

I accept that all that we need to achieve in life goes under at least one of the above classes. Here are a couple of instances of goals that may go under every classification:

1. Happiness: get a sweetheart, join an interest group

2. Health: run a long-distance race, cut out complex carbs

3. Success: be met on national TV, sell a business for six figures

4. Wealth: have $1m in the bank, claim a uniquely custom-fitted suit

5. Giving: tutor somebody, join an outside guide program

6. Growth: live in a remote nation, eat with a Nobel Prize champ

Try not to think that you recognize what you need tragically. Set aside some effort to think about every one of them over six classes, and make a list of everything that you need to achieve. List liberally, unpredictably, and egotistically. Take as much time as necessary.

This is your bucket list, and you will need to keep it close, as it should keep on developing for a mind-blowing remainder.

Here are a couple of things from my (relatively long) container list:

- Do a performance sky jump?
- Visit Yosemite National Park
- Write a distributed book
- Shake hands with a President
- Drive over the USA
- Help a decent aim with something other than cash

I realize that I won't accomplish everything on my list. Yet, I know that I will achieve a damn sight more by the way that I am deliberately mindful of them. There is incredible power in having something recorded.

Keep Goal Setting Simple

If you have followed my instructions, you will most likely presently have an impossibly overwhelming list of potential achievements. While it is critical to have this list, it is also a significant token of the fact that it is so natural to get overpowered when defining goals. What you totally should not do is attempt to take on more than you could deal with.

In light of that, I need you to select the one thing on that list that you think will have the best valuable effect on your life. It's hard to believe, but it's true, only one thing. Presently I need you to take as a lot of time as it is crucial to find out whether that goal merits coming to. Ask yourself the exceedingly important question:

"Will the essential exertion I need to place in to accomplish this goal be coordinated or surpassed by the gainful result?"

At that point, ask yourself the following questions:

1. Does the objective energize me?

2. Does the objective feel possibly extraordinary?

The response to the two inquiries ought to be an insistent, "Yes!"

What you have thought of is the thing that I like to call your "One Big Goal." It speaks to the single most significant contrast you can make to your life. If it doesn't, you ought to return to your list and ponder what you need from life. An obvious case of such an objective would be, "Quit my place of employment." That was my One Big Goal a year ago, the focal point of every one of my efforts. It felt big. It excited me, and I thought that it would be extraordinary (and it was). By now, you should have your One Big Goal.

Separate Your Goals

About achieving goals, the key is to separate them into little, practical, and actionable tasks. Your One Big Goal is probably going to look huge and scaring at face esteem, however like whatever else you do throughout everyday life, and its evident scale can be cut down to measure.

Objective Setting: How to Execute Your Next Steps

By this stage, you ought to have characterized your One Big Goal and separated it into reasonable advances. None of which is of any utilization except if you start executing.

To get directly to the point, expecting you have the necessary inspiration, executing is regularly the most direct piece of the procedure. When you realize what you need, and you realize how to get it, you should bear the cost of yourself an opportunity to complete the essential tasks. It might seem like I am misrepresenting the procedure, yet on a fundamental level, it's just as simple as that.

Your One Big Goal ought to be a focal component in your life, so you ought to experience little difficulty in discovering some time each day to move in the direction of it. I accept that is the situation for everybody. Sure — a few people will have additional time than others. However, for the individuals who are going to reveal to themselves that they mostly don't have time, with the best of regard, I call bullshit.

Regardless of how busy your life is, there are a million others out there as yet achieving more. That shouldn't debilitate you, or make you have a feeling that you are here and there lacking. Despite what might be expected, it should push you to coordinate their accomplishments.

The Importance of Regular Goal Setting Reviews

As I would see it, probably the most concerning issue with achieving goals is keeping your focus on the big picture. You may well have reliably pursued every one of my means up until this point. However, it will all be for nothing if you don't routinely audit what you are attempting to achieve, why, and how.

At the point when I state consistently, I mean week by week. Monday morning is a critical time for me. It is where I take an hour or so to help myself to remember what I am trying to achieve, why I am attempting to accomplish it, what I have achieved up until this point, and whether the work I am doing is taking me closer to that objective. I rehash this procedure for every one of the primary goals I am attempting to achieve (for example, "quit my place of employment," or "run a long-distance race").

The survey procedure ought to include the over four inquiries, and ought to be done recorded as a hard copy. So returning to my 2011 "quit my place of employment" goal once more, my Monday morning would've looked similar to this:

1. What am I trying to achieve? I am attempting to get into a position where I can leave my place of employment.

2. Why am I trying to make it? Since I need power over my salary and the opportunity to take a shot at my terms.

3. What have I met up until now? I have launched my blog and made some requests for employment.

4. How am I moving in the direction of my goal? Is it taking me closer to my objective, and provided that this is true, how? I am dealing with my blog and submitting employment forms. It is bringing me closer to my goal, since developing the blog will prompt more customer

referrals, and submitting applications will lead to jobs.

Each question has a reasonable reason:

1. Remind yourself of what you are trying to achieve.

2. Remind yourself of your reason for inspiration.

3. Assess your accomplishments to date, and give yourself a gesture of congratulations (or a kick up the ass).

4. Re-center around your activities, and whether you are on the best way to achieve your goal.

CHAPTER 5
DON'T START THE DAY UNTIL YOU HAVE IT FINISHED

No two circumstances are the equivalent; thus, numerous factors may not make this achievable in your very own life. For instance, I have no kids, stroll to and from work ordinarily, and have consistently been a morning individual.

The following is the framework that has worked for me.

Beginning Shift to Waking Up at 5 AM To Increase Productivity

As I suggested in my awakening at 5 AM post, I'd slipped into an ineffective propensity a couple of years earlier. My alarm in the first part of the day was being pushed later and later.

I was surging off to work, having achieved nothing in the first part of the day. When I came back following a busy, frequently distressing day at the workplace, my vitality level was low, and I'd either skip or put in a despicable exercise. Any considerations of side hustling, beginning a side business, or investigating new open doors was lost.

Long-story-short, the direction in numerous features of my life was going the incorrect way. There appeared to be a steady mentality of these people.

Win the morning, win the day.

That first 5 AM alert went off approx. Twenty-eight months prior and possesses remained bolted to that energy for 97% of the days since.

A Productive Day Starts the Night before – 5 Tips from My Routine

Time is a limited resource, and we are each lone given such a significant number of days, hours, minutes, and seconds to accomplish our objectives.

I've generally been a morning individual. Some of you may be more qualified to being night owls. Once more, no two circumstances are the equivalent. I've discovered that I'm generally beneficial in the mornings (outside of my descending direction period).

Along these lines, I'm hoping to utilize that time most adequately in 3 explicit zones. Those center focuses are wellness, side hustling (blog and freelance digital marketing), and getting ready for work.

The objective for me at that point is that when I wake up, I've set myself up for the most achievement conceivable.

1.) Organizing For Productivity

This phase of the prior night schedule can be nailed down to: perfect, spread out, and get ready.

The goal is too finished or set up any of the strategic, managerial, and lumbering errands the prior night, so I can use those most beneficial morning hours on what is essential most.

Planning Food to Help Morning Productivity

I carry my lunch to work 95% of the time (by and large 19 out of 20 days more than about a month). On Sunday,

I will mass cook dinners to cover Monday – Wednesday. At that point on Wednesday night, I do likewise to cover Thursday – Saturday.

Every night I bundle up my lunch for the following day with the goal that the main thing I have to do in the first part of the day is snatched it from the fridge.

For my morning nourishment and drink needs, each night, I will sort out my pre-exercise nibble and orchestrate my morning meal things to the front of the ice chest or pantry. Also, I get everything to make espresso out and set it next to the machine.

Dishes Clear For a Clear Mind

This was something my Mom ingrained in me. She used to state something along the lines of "a grimy dish in the sink is an elusive incline."

It might've been a ploy to get me to, in every case, tidy up after myself. However, what she indeed implied was having the attitude of "I'll do it later" was an elusive incline. Outside of dishes, that perspective can have an exacerbating negative impact.

In this manner, every single night, the sink is unfilled. The counter is evident outside of my espresso cup and water bottle.

Cloths Ready for a Productive Morning

The last unwieldy errand of setting myself up for a profitable morning is apparel. All the more explicitly, getting the garments out required the following day's exercise and time at the workplace.

These are hung and spread out each night.

Once more, I'm generally profitable in the first part of the day, so the objective here is to mitigate any unimportant projects as the most ideal. I can wake up to quickly put on my exercise outfit and again get changed for work after showering without putting thought on what to wear, discovering things, and so on.

I need to run on autopilot with regards to smaller choices so I can put most of the spotlight on that wellness, side hustle, and work prep needs.

2.) Reflecting On the Day

Every night as I'm slowing down, I set aside some effort to ponder the day that was. This, for the most part, happens after the minor prep tasks above are finished.

What worked out in the right way? Were there any close to home or professional successes to celebrate? Did anything not go as arranged? Is there something I fouled up to reason that?

Pondering back these insane, occupied, and quick-paced days encourages me to reset and reconnect with what I did (or didn't do). In some cases, the takeaways won't significantly affect anything. Different occasions, this procedure gives me a reasonable picture of bettering my life, money, profession, and relationships.

I go through 5-10 minutes, writing these down in a moleskin journal.

Journaling – Reflection for Productivity

I unquestionably wasn't generally somebody who wrote in a diary or spent whenever on self-reflection. Like the explanation I moved to awaken at 5 AM, I was hearing such a significant number of useful and intriguing individuals notice it as a feature of their daily procedure.

3.) Planning For a Productive Tomorrow

The following stage is laying the foundation for what I need to achieve the following day. The successes and misfortunes from the journaling stage 1 above regularly help build up these objectives and needs.

Realizing I have this 5 AM – 8 AM window before work to think with limited interruptions, I need to guarantee I recognize what I'm attempting to do.

Making arrangements for a profitable tomorrow has genuinely helped me take proprietorship and spike pledge to what I need to accomplish. In any case, composing these during the time before had additionally made my mornings increasingly streamlined as I comprehend what I'm hoping to concentrate on from the minute I wake up.

This is practiced through the journal again and the application Todoist.

Journaling – Goals, and Priorities

The following section in my moleskin journal after the day by day reflections area is the objectives and needs for the following day.

I will work out a wellness plan for the following morning. I've been doing this long enough since my various schedules are instilled in my mind. Yet, the demonstration of working it out truly fortifies that responsibility and responsibility.

Next up is the side hustle and blogging objectives and needs for the following morning. Since beginning this blog, I've moved my independent advanced advertising hours to half of what they used to be. I presently spend approx. One hour chipping away at each toward the beginning of the day after the exercise, shower, and breakfast.

At long last, I will make a note of any groups, ventures, up and coming cutoff times, or critical subtleties on the timetable or need a list for my work. Once more, this is to help set me up for progress the following day by effectively arranging and considering the coming day.

Todoist – Check Lists For a Productive Day

In the wake of making a note of this wellness, side hustle, and work objectives and needs by hand, I make some quick Todoist checklists on my telephone.

Todoist is a fantastic application and platform for sorting out, arranging, setting updates, and remaining on track.

The entire goal here is topping that responsibility, duty, and control to my most significant objectives and needs. It's likewise very satisfying to "verify" things on your plan for the day on Todoist.

Medium has an extraordinary element on mastering Todoist so you can best utilize the application.

4.) No Screens and Reading

Given my brand marketing career in a dynamic, continually evolving industry, side hustle advanced promoting projects and running this blog, I regularly don't hold up my finish of the deal with the 'no screen' rule.

However, an objective of mine is as far as possible my screen time before bed. I noted having an entire 24-hour advanced detox as one of the things on the 30 little successes challenge.

Getting Enough Sleep to Drive a Productive Morning

At the point when I initially fired awakening at 5 AM, I was resting 6 to 6.5 hours. Following nine months of that, I realized I expected to draw nearer to 7 hours reliably.

As of late, the objective is to be lights out and nodding off at 10 PM or prior. However, this is, as of now, another deficit that I'm effectively hoping to improve my consistency with.

I notice the distinction in profitability even when I get 7 hours 15 minutes versus 6 hours 45 minutes. To keep away from wear out and stay gainful, I have to guarantee I'm getting enough rest.

In Closing... A Productive Day Starts the Night Before

As I referenced before, no two circumstances are the equivalent. What is attainable and advantageous for my life may not thoroughly be appropriate to your way of life and living circumstances.

There are many systems, assets, and stunts that can expand efficiency.

By and by, I will likely use the morning as a chance to all the more likely to arrive at my objectives – monetarily, imaginatively, physically, etc. As of late, setting myself up for a productive morning has made significant energy by working out the framework above.

63% of respondents in an ongoing CareerBuilder study said they think "working nine-to-five" is an old idea, and 24% browse work messages while investing energy with loved ones. Those figures presumably won't shock anybody with a vocation in the advanced information economy. In any case, while versatile innovation has empowered us to work all the more deftly, it's additionally empowered a significant number of us to work more, period.

One motivation behind why is because we've figured out how to design less; we can generally monitor something remotely or run off a message on the fly. Luckily, a significant number of those equivalent advanced instruments can assist us with setting the phase to complete things the following day before we even set foot in the workplace, as long as we use them admirably the previous night—or previous.

1. USE TIME BLOCKING

Writing the main priority the last night is an incredible method to guarantee you start your workday strong. Sound simple? It is—yet it's something a large number of us have overlooked how to do. To make it a stride further, however, go your daily agenda into an undeniable timetable utilizing the time-blocking method?

Before you head to sleep, make a rundown of every one of your assignments, gatherings, and tasks for the day ahead. Start by sorting out your telephone assembles and conferences by time. From that point, you can fill in any free hours with the day's assignments arranged by need.

Before you go to bed, make a rundown of every one of your assignments, groups, and tasks for the day ahead.

This way to deal with sorting out your day maybe won't sound entirely adaptable. Yet, as a general rule, it prevents you from being responsive. Instead, it urges you to concentrate on the main job and opening whatever assignments that spring up into the free spaces of your day, as opposed to needing to drive different things aside to bounce on them. To assist you with adhering to your time squares, attempt an apparatus like StayFocusd, which causes you to limit the measure of time you spend tarrying around the internet, as indicated by restricts you can set ahead of time.

Also, something as necessary as a period blocking can spare you from passing up genuinely necessary rest. Rather than laying wakeful around evening time agonizing over what you have to complete the following day, make a rundown and put it to bed.

2. Assemble ROUTINES THAT CONSERVE YOUR BRAINPOWER

In case you're similar to a great many people, you have a morning schedule: wake up, shower, brush your teeth, have breakfast, and so forth. In any case, practically speaking, they never go as arranged.

That is the place innovation can help. There are

presently a few applications that can assist you in transforming your ordinary propensities into effective work processes. I thought places an awful preference for your mouth, think about what your day by day schedules are formed as of now—so why not streamline them? The Workflow application, for example, encourages you to locate the nearest spot to snatch espresso, keep away from traffic, and eventually get the opportunity to take a shot at a time, limiting how much time that entire routine takes up in your day in any case.

3. Separate YOUR DEADLINES

Planning out your following day the previous night sounds sensible enough to the more significant part of us (whether we do it), yet shouldn't something be said about your week, month, or year? With regards to monitoring deadlines, day by day plans for the day don't generally give you the full picture. Take a stab at separating those increasingly far off cutoff times into days.

As per one, an ongoing report distributed in Psychological Science, individuals who changed over their objectives and cutoff times from years into days were increasingly proactive about beginning on them. Schedule applications like Fantastical 2 can make that much more straightforward, adding suggestions to handle singular parts of longer-term extends early. Along these lines, you won't be left scrambling on the morning of a significant deadline.

4. Go to bed, ALREADY!

Like your parents consistently let you know, an ideal approach to ensure you have a good day is to get the opportunity to bed early. Some coffee can accomplish such a great deal following a late or fretful night.

Here is a portion of the bad before-sleep time habits you should consider curtailing:

• Too much trivial screen time, whether it's with your telephone, PC, or TV

• Checking messages, work or individual

• Having a nightcap

• Starting a book discussion that can hold up until the following day

• Skipping time to slow down

To ensure you're getting enough sleep in any case, take a stab at utilizing a rest following contraption like the Fitbit or an application like Sleep Cycle, intended to record your dozing propensities and give you a superior comprehension of the nature of rest you're getting.

At the point when you wake up, it won't merely feel like there's less for you to handle. There really will be.

Alan Carniol is the founder of Interview Success Formula, a program that causes work searchers to convey ground-breaking answers that demonstrate why they are the correct individual for the activity. He is an individual from the Young Entrepreneur Council (YEC), a just welcome association that involved the world's most encouraging young entrepreneurs.

Step by step instructions to Plan Your Day the Night Before

Since you know the significance of arranging, the following thing you have to do is the most pivotal part; you have to design.

So how would you plan your day, especially around evening time? Here are a few rules that you can pursue.

1. Remind Yourself to Plan

The first tip to arranging is to make sure to design. If you are not used to arranging, there is a high possibility that you will miss it.

You may have used to hit the sack after viewing the TV. So you don't have the propensity for arranging before you rest.

Also, for a great many people, whether they chose to design their previous day they hit the sack, they may neglect to do as such and rest straight away.

Consequently, you should remind yourself to design. And afterward, make it a propensity with the goal that you will do it each time before you go into your room.

Here are some smart thoughts that you can execute:

- Set the alarm to reveal to you it's an excellent opportunity to design. You can set it to 30 minutes before you rest or whatever that works for you.

- Put your note pad or your organizer someplace you can see it before you hit the hay. For instance, you can put it by your bed or someplace noticeable to you.

- Make arranging some portion of your evening rituals.

2. Distinguish Your Biggest and Ugliest Frog

The critical explanation you plan your day is that you need to be progressively beneficial and produce more outcomes in your day. Accordingly, you should distinguish your greatest and ugliest frog and eat it first.

Brian Tracy, the top of the line author of Eat That Frog, utilizes the representation of a frog as your undertaking. He says that you should eat the greatest and ugliest frog the first thing, which implies you should get the most significant and troublesome task done the first thing.

When you completed the most significant work, you will feel lighter and ready to experience the day with certainty.

Also, do recollect that your significant assignment must be the errand that gives you the most outcome that you want.

3. Plan Using the Pomodoro Technique

The Pomodoro Technique is a well-known time-the board method that you should execute. This procedure enables you to concentrate on your work and get rest to counteract burnout.

How it functions is essential. Mainly, you center on your labor for 25 minutes, and afterward, you take a 5 minutes rest. What's more, you rehash this procedure for around four sets, and afterward, you take a long 30 minutes break.

This will ensure you get enough rest with the goal that you can keep up your concentration at a more elevated level.

I think that it's hard to concentrate on one undertaking over quite a while outline because our minds need to rest, and we spent our self-control like our phone batteries.

At the point when you center and labor for 25 minutes, you will have the option to create an incredible outcome. Also, when you take a short 5 minutes break, you are reviving your mind and invigorate it.

4. Utilize the Time-Blocking Method

This is another powerful time management technique that will make you beneficial, and I unequivocally propose you utilize this method in your day.

At the point when you obstruct your time for a task, you are giving that assignment a continuous-time. For example, you can time-hinder an hour or two to compose articles for your blog or to cold pitch your possibilities.

I do this for composing the content of this blog. In any event, until further notice, as I'm writing this sentence, I'm doing it during my time-square period.

The way to fruitful time-square is to ensure you dispose of all the interruption and spotlight 100% on your work.

Furthermore, you should time-obstruct your most significant task with the goal that you can complete the most and produce the most outcome.

Attempt it, and you will perceive how incredible it is.

5. Write them down

This may sound too easy to even think about doing, and when things are excessively simple, individuals will, in general, overlook them. Never let its effortlessness fool you. You should record your plan.

It is doubtful you can recollect everything in incredible detail with your mind. You will overlook when there are interruptions.

So get yourself a good notebook. I get myself a decent journal or an organizer to do my arranging every year. I record my day by day tasks every week and survey the following day the prior night.

In any event, when I'm composing this, my organizer is perfect alongside my PC. At whatever point a thought runs over, I will record it into my organizer.

6. Schedule Some Fun

Never neglect to schedule some enjoyment into your day also. Neil Fiore, the well-known writer of the book, The Now Habit, proposes peruses plan fun time into their schedule first before they even put in their work.

The explanation is that you need to reveal to yourself that the prizes and the fun are there. What is the point if everything you do is work, work, and work without joy? Except if you are incredibly energetic about your work and you think that it's enjoyable to work, else you will feel that it's exhausting and hard to the direction of your vitality to experience your day without the good times.

So plan something fun as well. It very well may be your side interest; it tends to mess around, and so forth. Anything that makes you connected with and lively.

7. Never Overestimate Yourself

Perhaps the most significant misstep the vast majority make is that they overestimate themselves. It transpires as well. I record an excessive number of things that I need to achieve, and toward the day's end, I completed short of what I anticipated.

Never overestimate yourself and your time. We as a whole have just 24 hours per day, not to overlook that we spend very nearly 33% of an opportunity to rest, and there will be interruptions during the day also.

If you can get the three most significant assignments accomplished for the afternoon, you are doing great. Your tasks must be something meaningful that will push you ahead toward your objectives.

Less is the new more, and little is the new huge, my friend.

It isn't about the amount; it is about quality. For whatever length of time that you get the most significant errand that will yield you the most outcome done, you are doing incredible.

8. Discover What Works

For me, I favor the "Richard Branson style" of planning. I want to design utilizing a physical organizer or a scratch pad instead of depending on technology.

I'm not saying that you ought to pursue what I did. Instead, you should discover what works best for you. I like to utilize an iPad or plan using your telephone put it all on the line.

You can likewise utilize an electronic organizer, for example, Trello, if you need to. The key is to discover what turns out best for you. If you don't know what your best alternative is, explore different avenues regarding a couple, and you will know soon enough.

9. Plan and Schedule According to Your Peak Moment

If you need to deliver a stunning outcome, you should design your most significant work around your pinnacle hours, where you are the most gainful.

Everybody is unique. For me, my mornings are the best minute. I'm the most profitable, and there are genuinely no interruptions in the majority of my mornings.

However, I time-hinder my composing work in the first part of the day. Toward the evening, I, for the most part, plan for work that requires less of my imagination, for example, answering messages, planning reports on Facebook, perusing, learning, and so forth.

Lao Tzu said the above quote. You will end up being the most beneficial and fruitful when you get yourself. So plan your day as indicated by your strengths.

10. Reflect and Review

At long last, you should mirror your day and survey what you have done. It is highly unlikely you can tell if you are doing things right except if you do an after death, isn't that so?

To reflect and survey your day. Much the same as what Steve Jobs did. He investigated the mirror and posed himself this one inquiry every day:

"If today were the latest day of your life, OK, need to do what you're doing?"

Furthermore, he stated, "At whatever point the appropriate response has been no for an excessive number of days straight, I realize I have to change something."

What's more, this is one of the keys to his prosperity. Steve Jobs assessed his life and his work about what works and what doesn't, and he did it consistently.

At the point when you do this, you comprehend what you need, you would then be able to course-address yourself to arrive at your objectives, and you will improve every day to grow as an individual, in both your career/business and your life.

CHAPTER 6
EAT A FROG FIRST

How about we talk about the main efficiency tip you'll require, why it works, and what keeps us away from utilizing it reliably.

Profitability, Simplified

No compelling reason to coax this out. This profitability tip is precise: Do the most significant thing first every day.

Sounds straightforward. Nobody does it.

Much the same as Hemingway, who created a striking volume of high-bore work during his profession, you can gain astounding ground every day if you do the most significant thing first.

Why It Works

We regularly expect that profitability implies accomplishing more things every day. Wrong.

Productivity is completing important things reliably. What's more, regardless of what you are going after, there are just a couple of genuinely important things.

Being profitable is tied in with keeping up a consistent, average speed on a couple of things, not the most extreme speed on everything.

That is the reason this strategy is successful. If you do the most significant thing first every day, at that point, you'll generally complete something meaningful. I don't think about you, yet this is a serious deal for me. There are many days when I squander hours check off the fourth, fifth, or sixth most significant tasks on my daily agenda and never get around to doing the most significant thing.

As you'll see beneath, there is no explanation you need to apply this strategy in the first part of the day. However, I figure beginning your day with the most significant task offers some extra advantages over different times.

To start with, a resolution will, in general, be higher prior in the day. That implies you'll have the option to give your best vitality and exertion to your most significant assignment.

Second, in my experience, the more profound I get into the day, the more probable it is that startling undertakings will crawl into my timetable, and the more uncertain it is that I'll invest my energy as I had arranged. Doing the most significant thing first every day keeps away from that.

At long last, the human personality appears to detest incomplete tasks. They make an uncertain strain and inner pressure. At the point when we start something, we need to complete it. You are bound to complete an assignment in the wake of beginning it, so start the significant undertakings at the earliest opportunity. (Simply one more motivation behind why the beginning is a higher priority than succeeding.)

Why We Don't Do It

The vast majority invest the more significant part of their energy, reacting to another person's motivation than their own.

I think this is halfway a consequence of how we are

raised by society. In school, we are given assignments and advised when to step through our examinations. At work, we are doled out due dates and given desires from our bosses. At home, we have undertakings or errands to perform to think about our children and our accomplices. Following a couple of many years of this, it can turn out to be anything but difficult to go through your day, responding to the upgrades that encompass you. We figure out how to make a move as a response to the desires, requests, or needs of another person.

So usually, when it comes time to begin our day, it doesn't appear to be bizarre to open our email inbox, check our telephone, and search for our most recent walking orders.

I think this is a misstep. The errands allocated to us by others may appear to be critical; however, what is dire is only here and there significant. The significant projects in our lives are the ones that move our expectations, our fantasies, our manifestations, and our organizations forward.

Does that imply that we ought to disregard our obligations as guardians or representatives or residents?

Not. In any case, we as a whole need a reality in our days to react to our motivation, not somebody else's.

Not a Morning Person?

Does the word morning cause you to grieve? Does the morning sun help you to remember The Eye of Sauron? Would you be able to consider nothing more regrettable than beams of brilliant daylight spilling delicately onto your pillow?

No stresses, night owls.

As I examined the everyday propensities for many writers, specialists, and artists in Daily Rituals (book recording), I saw a significant pattern: There was no pattern.

There is nobody approach to be fruitful. There is similarly the same number of night owls delivering marvelous work as there is the brisk riser. In any case, regardless of what their specific routine resembled, each profitable artisan grasped, ensuring a sacrosanct time every day when they could take a shot at their motivation.

I discover morning to work best. Your mileage may differ.

The expression "Do the most significant thing first every day" is only a basic method for saying, "Give yourself a reality to take a shot at what is imperative to you every day."

If you need increasingly useful thoughts for bringing an end to adverse behavior patterns and making great propensities, look at book Atomic Habits, which will give you how little changes in tendencies can prompt surprising outcomes.

Like many individuals, I have a hurrying plan for the day that is sorted out by classification - customer, advertising, authoritative, and individual tasks. To test this methodology, I had first to conflict with my imbued propensity and made sense of which of the things was, truth be told, the most significant. Did I solicit myself - which from these things is going to have the most significant effect on developing my business?

This wasn't as simple as it ought to have been. I needed to put in a few minutes attempting to make sense of precisely what the crucial initial step was. I accept this problem is at the core of why we put off significant errands: When it comes to greater, progressively significant assignments, we're often not sure where to begin.

For this to work for me, I needed to separate large errands into increasingly significant pieces. It required asking myself, what is the littlest conceivable initial step I could take to get going on this project? When I had the option to venture out, second becomes evident and afterward, the third and fourth, etc.

Following three days of utilizing Justin's most significant project approach, this is what I found. Shock! It worked. I gained more and faster ground in building another assistance in my business than I'd envisioned I could. Be that as it may, as basic as this methodology seems to be, it requires discipline. Control is particularly extreme for me when the pace of customer work or family life gets, or when anything drops into my day startlingly, for example, a call from childcare to get a wiped out child.

This way, to deal with organizing your undertaking list with an extreme, essential spotlight on your most significant assignment can work for you as well. It's the main path any of us can make critical, quick progress towards our objectives. Reliably putting less significant errands further down on your daily agenda will have an enormous effect on your business development, income, and commitment with customers and staff.

Endorphins are synthetic compounds created generally by the sensory system to adapt to torment or stress. They are frequently called "feel-better" synthetics since they can go about as a torment reliever and joy booster.

Endorphins are primarily made in the nerve center and pituitary organs; however, they may originate from different pieces of the body also. The notable "sprinter's high" that is felt after prolonged, vivacious exercise is because of an expansion in endorphin levels.

The degree of endorphins in the human body differs from individual to individual. Individuals who have lower levels might be bound to have melancholy or fibromyalgia. However, more research is required there.

What are endorphins?

Endorphins are chemicals that help to assuage torment or stress, and lift satisfaction.

Endorphins are chemicals created by the body to

alleviate pressure and torment. They work comparable to a class of medications called opioids.

Opioids calm pain and can create a sentiment of rapture. They are, in some cases, endorsed for momentary use after a medical procedure or for help with discomfort.

During the 1980s, researchers were concentrating on how and why opioids worked. They found that the body has extraordinary receptors that quandary to opioids to square torment signals.

The researchers at that point understood that a few synthetic compounds in the body also acted to specific narcotic drugs, authoritative to these equivalent receptors. These chemicals were endorphins.

The name endorphin originates from the words "endogenous," which signifies "from the body" and "morphine," which is an opioid pain reliever.

A portion of the more typical opioid drugs include:

- Oxycodone
- Hydrocodone
- Codeine

- Morphine

- Fentanyl

Some illicit medications, for example, heroin, are additionally opioids. Both lawful and unlawful opioids prescriptions have a high risk of causing enslavement, overdose, and passing.

The National Institute on Drug Abuse express that 90 individuals bite the dust every day in the United States from opioids overdose. A significant number of these are an aftereffect of overdosing or abusing remedy narcotics.

Opioid abuse and overdose have become such a problematic issue, that the National Institutes of Health have pronounced it an emergency. Therapeutic specialists are currently investigating sheltered and compelling pain relievers without an opioid.

Healthy endorphins work comparatively to opioid torment relievers, yet their outcomes may not be as sensational. In any case, endorphins can deliver a "high" that is both solid and safe, without the risk of enslavement and overdose.

Boosting endorphins

The accompanying exercises show guarantee as approaches to normally expand endorphins. However, endorphin levels change between people, so results will likewise fluctuate.

Regular exercise

Regular exercise has been found to help battle tension and gloom because of the endorphins it discharges.

For quite a long time, researchers presumed that endorphins caused the supposed "sprinter's high," an inclination of happiness that occurs after protracted, enthusiastic physical movement.

However, estimating endorphins in people was impractical until 2008, when new imaging innovation got accessible.

Analysts utilized positron emission tomography (PET) sweeps to see competitor's minds both when working out. They found an expansion in the arrival of endorphins after exercise.

As exercise helps mindset and expands endorphins, some restorative experts endorse regular exercise as a treatment for mellow to direct gloom and tension.

Exercise can be utilized securely related to different medicines, for example, drugs or treatment, and can likewise be used alone. One investigation expresses that activity can improve a few indications of despair, comparable to antidepressants.

Giving

Volunteering, giving, and helping other people may likewise make an individual vibe great. Analysts at the National Institutes of Health found that individuals who offered cash to philanthropy enacted joy focuses on their brains. This may prompt improved endorphin levels.

Yoga and contemplation

Meditation and yoga are known for their pressure assuaging and loosening up impacts. This might be incomplete because of an endorphin release.

Some researcher recommends that yoga and

contemplation can diminish pressure markers and increase endorphins.

Spicy foods

Individuals who appreciate spicy foods may find that they can get an extra lift from their preferred dishes.

Some researchers propose that the hot segments in hot peppers and comparative foods may trigger a pain sensation in the mouth, which prompts an expansion in endorphins.

Dark chocolate

Research from 2013 proposes that eating dark chocolate could help endorphin levels. Cocoa powder and chocolate contain synthetic substances considered flavonoids that seem, by all accounts, to be valuable to the brain.

A 2017 survey found that eating chocolate may help support endorphins. Nonetheless, numerous business chocolate items contain just modest quantities of real cocoa and frequently contain liberal measures of included sugar and fat.

Individuals hoping to utilize chocolate to improve endorphin levels and state of mind should search for items that contain in any event 70 percent cocoa and eat chocolate with some restraint because of its unhealthy and fat content.

Laughing

A lot of research has been expounded on the medical advantages of giggling, and studies recommend that snickering builds endorphins.

A recent report found that social giggling discharges endorphins in mind.

Low endorphins and wellbeing conditions

At the point when endorphin levels are excessively low, an individual's health might be contrarily influenced. An examination of the connection between endorphins and health conditions is continuous.

A few examinations have indicated a potential connection between the following medical issues and low endorphin levels:

Depression

Without enough endorphins, an individual might be bound to have misery. An article in the American Journal of Psychiatry talks about the long-standing utilization of narcotic medicines for depression, especially in situations where different medications have not worked.

Another article recommends that higher endorphin levels affect misery side effects as a result of their association with reward.

Fibromyalgia

Basic symptoms of fibromyalgia include:

- Long-term pain all through the body
- Tender recognizes that hurt when they are touched
- Muscle stiffness
- Fatigue and low vitality
- sleep issues

Individuals with fibromyalgia may have lower than ordinary endorphin levels. One examination found that individuals with fibromyalgia had lower levels of endorphins than those without the condition. They estimated endorphins both when working out.

Another investigation found that increments in the body's endorphins were related to relief from discomfort in individuals with fibromyalgia.

Individuals with fibromyalgia might be encouraged to do specific exercises to help endorphins, for example, work out, interfacing with others, and stress-easing activities, for example, yoga. They may also be recommended prescriptions to help with side effects.

Chronic headaches

One potential reason for progressing cerebral pains is abnormal endorphin levels. Some exploration recommends that a similar endorphin irregularity that contributes to depression is also present in people who have chronic headaches.

Takeaway

The study of human endorphin levels is as yet developing, as specialists keep on studying this synthetic and how it influences overall health.

Individuals who have indications of melancholy, fibromyalgia, or constant migraines may wish to converse with a specialist about endorphin levels and ways they can expand them, also their regular treatment options.

While endorphins are not a "fix-all" or assurance of good health, boosting endorphins might be a powerful method to expand by and abundant prosperity.

Customary exercise, stress decrease, and providing for others are outstanding "feel-better" exercises that can enable an individual to carry on with a healthier and happier life.

The endorphin "high" is a lovely reward that may enable an individual to adhere to these great habits.

We probably won't have a cash tree. However, we can have a satisfaction tree. Dopamine, serotonin, oxytocin, and endorphins are a group of four answerable for our joy.

Numerous occasions can trigger these synapses, but instead of being in the front seat, there are ways we can deliberately make them flow.

Being in a positive state has a critical effect on our inspiration, efficiency, and prosperity. No reasonable individual would be against having more elevated levels in those areas.

Here are some basic approaches to hack into our positive neurochemicals:

Dopamine

Dopamine motivates us to make a move toward objectives, wants, and needs, and gives a flood of strengthening delight while achieving them. Stalling, self-uncertainty, and absence of energy are connected with low degrees of dopamine. Studies on rats indicated those with lesser degrees of dopamine consistently decided on a simple choice and less nourishment; those with more elevated levels applied the exertion expected to get double the measure of nourishment.

Separate enormous objectives into little pieces as

opposed to possibly enabling our minds to celebrate when we've hit the end goal, we can make a progression of small end goals which discharges dopamine. And, it's urgent to celebrate purchase a container of wine, or head to your preferred café at whatever point you meet a small goal.

Rather than being left with a dopamine aftereffect, make goals before achieving your present one. That guarantees a constant flow for experiencing dopamine. As a business and pioneer, perceiving the achievements of your group, for example, sending them an email, or giving a reward, will enable them to have a dopamine hit and increment future inspiration and efficiency.

Serotonin

Serotonin streams when you feel huge or significant. Loneliness and depression show up when serotonin is missing. It's maybe one motivation behind why individuals fall into packs and crime. The way of life brings experiences that encourage serotonin release. Unhealthy attention-seeking behavior can also be a weep for what serotonin brings. Princeton neuroscientist Barry

Jacobs clarifies that most antidepressants center on the generation of serotonin.

Thinking about past significant achievements enables the mind to re-live the experience. Our mind experiences difficulty differentiating between what's genuine and imagined, so it produces serotonin in the two cases. It's another motivation behind why appreciation practices are widespread. They advise us that we are esteemed and have a lot to an incentive throughout everyday life. On the off chance that you need a serotonin help during a stressful day, take a couple of seconds to consider past accomplishments and triumphs.

Eat or espresso outside and open yourself to the sun for 20 minutes; our skin ingests UV beams, which advances nutrient D and serotonin generation. Although an excessive amount of bright light isn't great, someday by day introduction is beneficial to support serotonin levels.

Oxytocin

Oxytocin makes closeness, trust, and assembles sound connections. People discharge it during the climax, and by moms during labor and breastfeeding. Animals will reject their posterity when the arrival of oxytocin is blocked. Oxytocin expands loyalty; men in monogamous connections who were given an increase in oxytocin associated with single ladies at a more prominent physical separation then men who weren't given any oxytocin. The development of oxytocin is fundamental for making strong bonds and improved social interactions.

Frequently referred to as the nestle hormone, a primary method to keep oxytocin streaming is to give somebody an embrace. Dr. Paul Zak clarifies that between close to home touch raises oxytocin; however, lessens cardiovascular pressure and improves the insusceptible framework, as opposed to only a handshake, go in for the embrace. Dr. Zak prescribes eight embraces every day.

At the point when somebody gets a blessing, their oxytocin levels can rise. You can fortify work and individual connections through a simple birthday or anniversary gift. Goleman further clarified that "the mesolimbic dopamine framework associates ... the orbitofrontal cortex, in the prefrontal region behind the forehead, with the amygdala in the brain's middle, and with the [nearby] nucleus acumens. Humans experiencing serious happiness identified with the strict practice were contemplated in explore revealed in the BBC exceptional, "All in the Mind: Understanding the Complexity of the Brain." They found a zone in the prefrontal cortex was enormously actuated during times of extraordinary religious devotion.

A long-time back, Nancy Reagan looked to reduce the effect of illegal medication use by urging us, "Simply state no!" A superior trademark maybe, "Don't simply disapprove of medications express yes to something better." Or, as the Apostle Paul put it, "Be not tanked with wine, yet be loaded up with the Spirit." An elective sort of intoxication has been known for a considerable length of time, and such elective poisonings have been designated "positive" addictions.

Indeed, even a basic brain science course will take note of that making a behavior vacuum doesn't work. That is the reason discipline is less successful than reinforcing an alternative behavior. The human or other creature with a conduct void will return to what is known, the first behavior. A positive compulsion, however, can replace a destructive addiction.

The Runner's High

Therapist William Glasser, in his book "Positive Addiction," extolls the sprinter's high, delivered by a natural hormone with opium-like impacts, released by the mind. Sprinters become dependent on the hormone and experience withdrawal impacts when an injury prevents running. And, that is the drawback. Runners have become so addicted that they run even though they realize it has gotten perilous. Death from a heart attack has resulted.

In any case, as Glasser notes, such constructive addictions as running and contemplation leave individuals progressively compelling and energetic. As one sprinter put it, "I have such a great amount to do, I don't have time not to run today."

Music, Performance, and Individual Forms of Positive Addiction

We all can locate our types of constructive compulsion, our particular manners of getting "high." People frequently give models from their very own lives.

Artists report euphoria from their versions of incredible music, and entertainers experience happiness when the audience applauds an excellent performance.

Dependence on Excellence and to Work

Alice Fisher, my instructor year's back, asked "addiction to excellence." For her and others, such a craving prompted excellent execution. Also, with other positive addictions, nonetheless, there is a peril; for this situation, compulsiveness. Perfectionists often are impeded by their addiction. They may get themselves unfit to work on the off chance that they can't be impeccable in their exhibition, or they may not submit amazing work they consider not good enough.

A related type of enslavement is a need to work, only for the delight it brings. As an HR supervisor, before starting my doctoral investigations, this was of extraordinary interest to me. I've asked whether the word obsessive worker is an unjustifiable put-down of individuals who buckle down or whether such individuals endure a dependence on work comparable to alcoholism. Once in a while, the appropriate response is, "Both."

Those who consistently work hotly from daybreak to 12 PM yet experience delight instead of depletion are, in reality, dependent. Their brains release opium-like synthetics, creating a high. If they decrease the power of their work, they suffer withdrawal similar to that of a cocaine addict. However, workaholic addiction can be a constructive alternative to destructive drug addictions.

I'm used to connecting 'happy highs' to outside things; however, scholastic Loretta Breuning, creator of Meet Your Happy Chemicals, says there's essential non-scholarly neurochemistry in every one of us behind these emotions, which is their main thrust. Basically, 'your brain spurts upbeat synthetic compounds which reward you with nice sentiments when you achieve something it sees as useful for your survival.'

We have two diverse brain frameworks – the limbic framework and the cortex – which keep us alive and secure our DNA. The limbic structure delivers the neurochemicals that mention to your body what's positive or negative for you. It's a survival mechanism: within sight of something great, the mind discharges four principles' feel good' synthetic compounds – endorphin, oxytocin, serotonin, and dopamine – and within sight of risk, the 'terrible inclination' concoction – cortisol – comes in.

As people, we have a huge cortex, which means we can abrogate 'animal' impulses. However, the limbic framework will continue tripping. 'At the point when we have a happy experience, the chemicals are processed; at that point, the bad emotions return, and despondent synthetics spread to occupy that space, so then we need to trigger more happy chemicals,' says Breuning.

In this way, we're secured in happiness-chasing because these concoction floods mean we always need to discover better approaches to get a fix. This isn't down to singular 'weakness,' includes Breuning: 'This hedonistic treadmill is completely normal and not something we're fouling up.' So, how would you help them?

1. Trust and having a place: Oxytocin is the 'holding' substance. If your trust has been sold out, you'll keep down, which can leave you inclining that you don't have a place. Build more trust by:

Being reliable. If others realize they can trust you,

you're bound to feel you can trust them.

I am finding an intermediary. Trust sets aside some effort to manufacture, so you could get a pet that will be faithful, join a gathering where you won't be judged, or play a game where you can share high points and low points.

You are having a massage. Setting aside an effort to apply body salve or face cream can also have any effect on feelings of wellbeing. As contact invigorates oxytocin, be progressively 'cuddly' with your partner, companions, or family, as well.

Counting your change. Check your trust. This causes you to get ready to fabricate trust with outsiders as opposed to remaining with who you know.

2. Rapture and assurance: Endorphin is nature's relief from pain – it's stimulated by pain. It developed for endurance; we need it to turn on and off, so we don't end up walking on a broken leg, for instance. Locate the perfect add up to push you through pain and promote wellbeing.

Laugh. A genuine belly laugh will 'shake up' your

internal parts positively. Real laughing (which makes your face ache) is thought to release fear.

Cry. Keeping down tears can develop pressure, while if you let it go when you have to, it's real help from strain for the most part in the body, and particularly in the stomach.

Exercise. In any case, change it around, as working similar muscles prompts mileage or damage. Feeling uncoordinated is the point – 'new' development is how you get the endorphin surge. Make it fun, with the goal that you snicker simultaneously.

Stretch. It's an extraordinary method to help the course. Attempt a yoga or Pilate's class, which will go considerably more in-depth. The thought is to extend those muscles you never at any point realized you had.

3. Inspiration: Dopamine encourages us to release the energy we have to get the prizes we need. In survival terms that typically means food and water, yet we can profit by it in different manners:

Take small steps. Breaking down an extreme errand you need to complete makes it feel more do-capable.

Your cerebrum will compensate you with dopamine each time, helping you achieve the goal.

Do a victory dance. Praising yourself on any little accomplishment will make you feel better. It probably won't give you the huge flood a long-distance runner gets crossing the end goal; however, it feels far superior to one-upmanship.

Raise the bar gradually. Regardless of the amount you need to, it's challenging to go from not cooking to regularly facilitating a major supper gathering. Make your objective practical in the first place and work from that point.

Act. Put aside 10 minutes per day to work on concrete actions, and dopamine will assist you with creating the energy to do as such.

4. Safety and respect: serotonin in a warm-blooded animal, serotonin is discharged when it sees it's more significant or more grounded than another; having a favorable position makes a sentiment of security. Social acknowledgment can be transient and eccentric. However, you can discover great courses to a sense of

pride:

Enjoy where you are. It's not in every case best to be in the driving seat, so realize that when will generally be glad to be the traveler. Status goes here and there.

Notice your impact. Without being controlling or arrogant, you can see when individuals have taken your lead. Try not to anticipate credit, set aside an effort to value your great impact on others.

Surrender control. A significant part of the time, we can't control what's going on, and that can be a considerable source of frustration. Pick one control 'habit' you have and attempt to release it along these lines, no checking the climate or taking a look at the clock.

Take pride. Decide to state 'look what I've managed' without being excessively tied up with the response – acknowledge that it may not generally be the one you need.

In case you're even remotely intrigued by profitability, you've heard this counsel a thousand times — start your workday with your first need. And if you've attempted to pursue this counsel, you realize it makes you progressively profitable.

It works for some reasons:

- We get fewer breaks in the first part of the day
- We have more self-discipline/discipline toward the beginning of the day
- If we finish the hard undertaking first, the accompanying simpler errands feel like a prize

However, if you've attempted to begin with your MIT (most significant task), you know it is quite tricky. Of course, you can do it for a day or two, or perhaps seven days. In any case, following half a month, you're back in your old example. Doing occupied work in the first part of the day and what feels speedy and straightforward, rather than what is significant.

It's not your flaw; however, that is precisely how our brains are wired — to search for the easiest course of action.

As far as I can tell, trying to say to yourself, "I'll do it" doesn't work at any rate, not long-term. What works is setting up a framework that will compel you to begin your day with your MIT.

We should investigate a couple of frameworks that will assist you in doing this long haul without teaching yourself and use resolution.

1. Set ONE Priority toward the END of Your Workday

Two significant focuses here:

1) Set just a single considerable task to deal with toward the beginning of the day and

2) Set it on the day preceding

If you pick an undertaking that is extremely significant for you, it will most likely be a difficult one. Regardless of whether it's only one, it will presumably be bounty to involve your morning time.

If the task is only one, you don't have the choice to procrastinate with more straightforward to do, less significant tasks. You have only one activity in the first part of the day and no reasons. No supports.

If you set the MIT toward the finish of your workday for tomorrow, it encourages you to unwind, let go of work, and make the most of your night realizing that everything is dealt with until tomorrow. At that point, when you wake up, you don't need to make any arrangements or timetables, start with your MIT.

2. Imprint Your Mornings as "Occupied" On Your Calendar

Ensure that your time is saved, and no one can "book" you while you're doing your MIT.

Regardless of whether you don't utilize a schedule, you can tell everyone that regularly intrudes on you; this is not a decent time for you.

Also, this helps program your brain that the morning is saved for efficiency. No busy work, no socializing, no procrastination, no funny business. Just the MIT until it's done.

3. Utilize an App to Get Rid of Distractions

These days it's anything but difficult to set up a couple of basic applications that will assist you with disposing of everything being equal and hold you in line. I prescribe two sorts of applications: web/telephone blockers, and social responsibility.

Web/Phone blockers

Except if there is something set up to keep you from getting diverted, you presumably will. Try not to try to utilize your self-control when it's such a significant amount of simpler to set up an application. Here are the applications that I prescribe:

- iPhone/Mac/Windows: freedom.to
- Android: focusme.com

I need a web association while you work, the apps let you square just specific sites and portable applications that are distracting.

Social Accountability

It's such a great amount of simpler to defer and stall when you're not responsible to anybody. Regardless of whether you have a chief or someone to answer to, regularly, that report is on a day by day or a week after week premise. As a rule, no one considers us responsible for being there toward the beginning of the day, start on schedule, and work on the best thing.

Also, the issue is even worse if you work for yourself, and you have no one to answer to. That is the reason for setting up social responsibility with somebody is essential.

An incredible application that I found as of late is focusmate.com.

How it works is, you plan a date and time on the application, and you get coordinated with an "efficiency mate." Your mate is odder that also needs to work in a concentrated manner around then. During the booked period, you both appear on camera, share for a moment or so what your most significant task is, and start working.

Your camera should be on during the session, so if you abruptly vanish without notice and a valid justification, your mate can consider you responsible.

For me, that is an incredible framework that consistently works. I realize that if I plan a gathering with somebody, I will be there. Without fail, on schedule, since I would prefer not to stand somebody up.

4. The Productive Morning Starts On the Night Before

One thing that can spoil every one of your arrangements is the absence of rest. If you don't head to sleep on schedule and get a lot of rest on the night before, your morning will most likely be wasted.

Regardless of whether you figure out how to get up on schedule and work on your task, your efficiency while you're restless will suck.

So if you set up a web-blocking application, a smart thought is to remember your nights for the blocking time frame as well. That way, you don't get diverted viewing YouTube late around evening time or get an irregular telephone call that goes on until 2 AM.

5. Set up Your Workstation for A Fast Start

One extra "ninja" stunt you can utilize is the point at which you're accomplished for the workday, pause for a moment to set up your workstation, so it's all set for tomorrow's MIT session.

If you have a devoted work PC, that is simple. Open

up the applications/sites/programming that you need and close everything random. At that point, put the PC to rest (or rest), with the goal that when you open it up on the following morning, there are no interruptions, and you're all set.

If you don't have a dedicated PC, it's a smart thought to make two client accounts — one for work, one for relaxation. Then you can easily remove everything distracting from the stir record and set it up for profitability for the first part of the day.

Regardless of whether your MIT isn't on a PC, you can, in any case, set up your workspace for a quick start. For example, tidy up your work area, get every one of the books and diaries that you need, and open them up on the correct page.

CHAPTER 7
ALLOCATE TIME IN CATEGORIES

The importance of time management

Many individuals accept they can't arrive at their dreams, travel to fascinating areas, land their dream jobs, finish their activities before the cutoff time, get enough rest each night, and invest enough energy with friends and family since they need more time.

In any case, here's the deal:

It's not constrained to time; that is the issue, its lousy time management.

What is effective time management?

Powerful time management is the viable utilization of your time that enables you to design your days so that you finish your work with less effort and benefit as much as possible from the limited time you have.

The significance and destinations of time the board is apparent in the advantages of powerful time management:

The advantages of time management or why time management is significant.

Realizing how to deal with your time appropriately is significant as it carries various incredible advantages to your work routine and life in general:

It causes you to achieve what you need, and quicker

At the point when you understand the significance of time management, you gain the inspiration to quit lounging around and seek after your goals.

Because of this challenging work and freshly discovered inspiration, you arrive at your goals faster.

It causes you to achieve more, yet in less time

At the point when you appropriately oversee time, you

accomplish more, yet additionally, spare more opportunity for exercises you genuinely appreciate.

When you properly manage time, state 60 minutes to a task and sticking to your plan will have a superior impact than chipping away at an assignment with no predefined time slot.

It causes you to burn through less time, and keep away from more contact and issues

Appropriately managing time incorporates making a plan for the day, allotting time to everything from your daily agenda, and then planning those assignments on your schedule.

Like this, you'll never again be indecisive about what you need to do next, and whether you'll need to complete all that you have to.

It causes you clear your timetable for more relaxation time, and feel more energized

Taking into account that appropriate time management causes you to finish your work faster, you'll see that you currently have all the more leisure time as a result.

All the more extra time will mean you have more

opportunity to go through with your friends and family, practice a hobby, or even go out traveling abroad – which will all bring about you feeling more energized.

The significance of time management in the working environment

Time the board is significant in life, generally speaking; however, it's particularly significant in the work environment. By appropriately dealing with your time, you'll see an extraordinary number of advantages:

You won't miss deadlines and appointments

Deadlines and appointments are regularly hard to monitor, and they're additionally barely noticeable, in case you're not careful.

To keep yourself on track with your work and finish on schedule, you have to ensure you start on schedule, and you'll also need to guarantee you separate your work into sensible pieces you'll have the option to handle in the predefined periods.

You'll concentrate more and procrastinate less

At the point when you realize you're dealing with a fixed calendar with tasks apportioned to a specific time in the day, it'll be simpler for you to the center because you'll realize you have specific cutoff times to meet for each task.

Thus, you'll postpone deal with said tasks significantly less.

You'll avoid unwanted stress

Racing to beat a cutoff time is distressing because you don't know whether you'll succeed. But, a great time, the Board encourages you to see your workday, not in general, yet as a lot of assignments you have to experience.

When you have every one of your tasks spread out that way, with the particular time you'll have to complete every one of them, it gets simpler to single out needs and make courses of action that ensure you limit such pressure.

You have doubtlessly heard it previously - recall your time following! Possibly you wonder why? This is similarly essential to everyone in an association or society when all is said in done. Regardless of whether you're an official, a chief, or a standard colleague, knowing where your time goes is paramount.

Time following is vital to seeing how you invest your energy, by and by, and in business. It is critical to profitability, knowledge, and a healthy workflow. At the point when you realize which tasks take the vast majority of your time, you can start to consider whether that time is all around spent. The most tedious tasks are not the tasks that require the most exertion to finish or bring the most worth. Regularly, a remarkable opposite.

Ask Yourself

• Did the task progress in the direction of a more extensive objective? (e.g., the business' crucial)

• And, is the task sufficiently significant to occupy that measure of time?

• Could the time have been all the more successfully spent and useful for an increasingly significant task?

- Did the assignment move in the direction of an individual or profession objective?

- Which stable changes carried out the responsibility make?

At the point when you are fearless, these questions covered it's a great opportunity to think about in the case of something could be improved, making your work process increasingly productive and successful. Could the work be re-sorted out to the better, does the product or equipment need an update, did you experience that you expected to look out for someone, or something, to continue? What annoyed you all the while? Change it. These are exceptionally significant questions to pose to both yourself and your group. Rank the assignments depending on the significance and designate your time appropriately.

Organize Your Time

Utilizing two measurements to examine your tasks is valuable.

1. To what broaden will the task benefit the organization or association, e.g., as far as benefits?

2. And, to what degree would we say we are ready to use on this assignment?

These two measurements will disclose to us whether every individual assignment is inside the extent of our business and if we can tackle the issue and rival rivals in the field. Errands scoring high on the two measurements, and lining up with the business technique, are the tasks to organize in your everyday work.

Advantages of Time Tracking

There are a few advantages of doing your time following, including;

• Personal and business bits of knowledge into time spent.

• Learning as a matter of fact and expanding profitability.

• Improving effectively and proficiency through learnings.

• Quality upgrades, following a streamlined work

process.

- Transparency into work forms.
- Cost productive conveyance on the center exercises.
- Ability to reflect and adjust in like manner.

The bits of knowledge you get from time following can regularly be an eye-opener. The amount of your time do you spend, perusing the web, looking through your inbox, or attempting to locate that one report in a heap of organizers. These are regularly seen as minor day by day exercises; however collected, these exercises are presumably the absolute most tedious exercises in your workweek is that supported?

Individual Time Tracking

Several software solutions look to facilitate the revelation of your digital time spent. RescueTime is one model that can follow your digital time across devices. Which sites and applications would you say you are regularly utilizing, and what amount? The time is then arranged and exhibited insignificant bits of knowledge with a general profitability score. In light of this score, you can contrast your workday from the week with week, gain as a matter of fact, and adjust your work process as needs are.

Those tools work extraordinary for a single time following, or little groups yet aren't ready to scale and are productive enough for a group of 10+, 100s, or perhaps 1000s of colleagues. The arrangements come up short on the immediate association with projects and tasks and aren't joined with other essential information, for example, your timetable and assets. It's not viable in such conditions.

Project Time Tracking

Nonetheless, a choice that is increasingly valuable for more significant associations is to do time following tracking directly on tasks. This is regularly done through a joined task and resource management solution. These make it simpler to deal with the entirety of your tasks across projects, and the association, to furnish you and your group with important bits of knowledge to manage time better.

The Digital Project Manager, the world's biggest online asset for digital project managers, has consolidated a specialist audit on the 10 Best Time Tracking tools, underscoring the significance of the exact timesheet detailing and the following spending consume. One choice for a potential arrangement, the Digital Project Manager, picked, is forecast.

Forecast makes time tracking relevant and straightforward by utilizing artificial intelligence to predict future time estimations. Time is accounted for legitimately on each task by each colleague, and the product tries to remember recorded information for the next counts to improve time estimations. Bits of knowledge is consequently produced through unique continuous announcing and introduced visually straightforwardly in the framework. Enabling you to get a more in-depth, objective, investigate your association to follow up on.

Time spent is a crucial proportion of resources required. It shows whether a division needs more assets, as far as workforce or different sources of info, and it gives you experiences on who carries the most incentive to the group. This is necessary data for the group, and the association, all in all. It may be the case that one individual does the vast majority of the work. In that circumstance, possibly something should be changed to carry everyone to a similar level, e.g., redistribution or sharing of obligation and the remaining task at hand.

Possibly someone's inclinations and inspiration has changed and would like to be migrated to another group in another division, bringing enthusiasm and development once again into their expert life, while pushing your business ahead. These are a portion of the bits of knowledge somewhat brought to the table by your time following endeavors and being occupied with your association.

CHAPTER 8
DO THINGS THAT HAVE LONG TERM GRATIFICATION

Have you at any point ended up needing to begin a task, to wind up surfing the net for a considerable length of time? Or then again, you need to eat more advantageous, however consistently end up getting the cheap food that is near you? It turns out there's a logical purpose for our battle between momentary rewards and long-term goals.

The two conflicting brain regions

According to research from Princeton University, there are two regions of the mind: one that is related to our feelings and the other with theoretical thinking.

As you would have guessed, the emotional piece of our mind reacts emphatically to moment delight. At the point when given the decision of cake now or broccoli later as your decision to eat more advantageous, this piece of your brain pushes you to pick the cake.

The logical part of your brain, however, attempts to prevail upon you. It may reveal to you that the broccoli is better for your long-term health and that you truly don't have to eat that chocolate cake. The feeling and rationale based pieces of your mind are always in a fight, attempting to give you why you ought to pick one alternative and not the other. So which part of our brain wins at last? It relies upon the situation. The specialists inferred that rash decisions happen when the passionate piece of our brains triumphs over the legitimate one.

At the point when individuals get truly near to obtaining a reward, their passionate brain dominates. So if a chocolate cake is gazing directly at you, things will get uncertain.

"Our emotional brain makes some hard memories envisioning the future, even though our consistent mind observes the future results of our present activities," says Laibson at Harvard University. "Our emotional brain needs to maximize the MasterCard, request pastry, and smoke a cigarette. Our consistent cerebrum realizes we should put something aside for retirement, go for a run, and stop smoking." At the point when we see, contact, or smell something that we truly need, the enticement is too extraordinary even to consider resisting. We act hastily because the dopamine in our cerebrums gets all started up. At the point when our mind has quieted down a while later, however, we wind up regretting our activities.

How to calm your brain and make the right choices

While we have the reasonable side of our brain to enable us to out, we can, in any case, effectively wind up settling on decisions that don't work in our long-term interests. So here are four strategies you can use to enable your cerebrum to mind give a valiant effort over the long-term:

1. Deal with your condition.

I've seen that longings frequently happen when I see an article. Since I've put healthier snacks and food close by, I don't have to consume energy attempting to oppose enticement.

Dealing with your surroundings additionally works when you need to achieve a significant objective. For example, if I need to read a book, I'll put it in a convenient spot (for example, close to my PC). Making your errands simple to get is the initial move towards getting increasingly profitable.

2. Tend to basic needs.

If conceivable, discover approaches to work with the enthusiastic side of your mind. If your brain is pushing you towards something, it may be a pointer of your energy levels.

Feeling tired? Sleep or get more rest. Protesting stomach? Eat adjusted dinners for the day. Cranky from stress? Proceed to play. At the point when your energy levels aren't being dealt with, your mindset drops, and your thinking skills worsen.

3. Tie emotion to your goals.

Our feelings can, without much of a stretch, overwhelm any rational conclusion abilities we have. So if you truly need to begin making a habit, at that point, partner it with a feeling. For example, if you continue putting off your thought, help yourself to remember the real prizes you'll experience if you begin.

4. Do what needs to be done.

At the point when we feel nervous or scared of doing something, we regularly attempt to convince ourselves to turn out to be progressively sure. While this technique assists support with increasing our confidence, there comes a moment that you need to bounce. Feeling free to give something a shot might be the confidence-booster you have to do it again later on.

Factors outside of thinking determine our choices. Interruptions and feelings can lead us away from where we need to go. In any case, on the off chance that you can discover approaches to get your brain to collaborate and carry on as indicated by your goals, at that point, you're well on your path to tipping the scales back in support of you.

The way to achieving long-term goals is finding the motivational tools that enable us to make little strides towards higher targets.

Moment delight is enticing and, these days, energetically feasible.

We approach everything data, nourishment,

innovation, diversion, comfort quickly. We don't need to apply a great deal of exertion into satisfying our wants, and, by and large, we can buy merchandise and projects in a moment that will delight all our necessities. What we don't consider are the exercises and advantages we pass up when we don't defer satisfaction. We experience self-improvement when we work more diligently to accomplish fulfillment. We additionally underestimate the benefit of focusing on long-term goals and drawing profit by the procedure by which we arrive at satisfaction.

Moderate blogger and creator Leo Babauta from zenhabits.net says that we don't need to deny ourselves of the beneficial things in life to achieve balance. It's only a question of restriction and care, being conscious about the choices we make, and having limits.

In an extravagance and innovation-focused world, it is anything but difficult to get disengaged from our guiding principle and the important things throughout everyday life. We begin to offer need to superficial things: objects, material riches, procurement, and appearance. We dispose of the need to recognize the future and potential ramifications for our activities. We don't think about waste, harm to our health or the earth, or other conceivable adverse impacts of our quick activities.

Our disappointment with short-lived pleasure makes our needs be amplified whenever we look for satisfaction. This can regularly prompt appalling and, to a great extent, unexpected costs like dependence. There are numerous instances of this. Overindulging in food, liquor or medications, innovation, for example, the web, gaming, and betting, even innocuous guilty pleasures like shopping or self-perception through diet and wellness can become fanatical and have counterproductive outcomes. That doesn't mean we need to dispose of our chances to appreciate these things. We need as far as possible, and we should know about how we get things done and how a lot or how regularly we enjoy.

Leo Babauta depicts five simple plans to assist us with resisting the desire to focus on moment delight. Rather than abiding in need to enjoy quick joy, he proposes approaches to remain careful and in charge. This will enable us to think about the long haul wants we can achieve, rather than requiring constant stimulation.

Being aware of the urges we experience is essential.

He recommends keeping a physical list of each time we get the desire to do something and, rather than satisfying it, merely making a note of it. Instances of these desires incorporate snacking, checking your phone, or buying something unnecessary.

He also brings up that as opposed to denying your desires totally, defer the delight. Put a timeframe, some space between when you feel an inclination and when you delight it.

The key is to rehearse cognizance and sharpen your familiarity with what's going in your brain and your body. We some of the time enjoy inclinations without intuition, and before we realize it, we've eaten up the whole tub of dessert or put another $1000 in a poker machine. If that is what you need to do, at that point, fine, do it; however, realize that what you are doing is a mindful choice and claim it. Assume liability for it.

These skills take practice, and it is imperative to enable yourself to learn exercises in a great time. If moment satisfaction has been your lifestyle for quite a while, don't anticipate that it should change medium-term. Improve with each experience. Allow yourself to fall flat and attempt to improve whenever a chance to practice resistance and care tags along.

At last, you will have the quality and control to appreciate the minute without really reveling the inclination. It gives us an incredible feeling of achievement and achievement when we understand how proficient we are of practicing resolution. These abilities can be incredibly fulfilling, and some of the time lifesaving, stopping smoking is an unmistakable model that rings a bell.

Putting resources into our future is underrated. With center and repetition, we can figure out how to anticipate long-term goals and limit our requirement for moment delight. We can discover any adjustment and still have the option to appreciate the best things in existence without overindulging and settling on choices that will influence our lives unfavorably.

CHAPTER 9
SET UP A FINISH LINE

Having goals is a crucial segment of inspiration. My default setting is to consider goals something new and harder than anything I've done previously. I ought to consistently be attempting to show signs of improvement, isn't that so? Be that as it may, is that truly obvious? Do objectives always need to be about progress? What happens when goals are about support? How might you make objectives for yourself that keep you engaged with a movement?

Perhaps the most significant test of hitting goals is the great marvel that as we arrive at 70%/80% of the target, individuals, especially salesmen, appear to back off. Maybe it's the fatigue and the work and exertion that has been placed in so far in hitting what they've just hit. It's a weird thing yet in a lot of organizations I've worked for. They consider hitting 80% in addition to a goal to be 'sufficiently close' in a ton of cases. A model was an innovation organization that, in reasonableness had extreme focuses on that they didn't anticipate that individuals should hit inevitably, however as opposed to defining the goal lines lower with the goal that you could feel a feeling of achievement at hitting your figures toward the month's end, they purposely set them to be testing.

What was the logic behind this, and how could the sales rep, or for sure anybody focusing on an objective, change themselves to ensure that they are hitting that very slippery 100%? Several exciting things were impacting everything here. The project lead checked any individual who achieved anything above 80% as being in the green every day refreshes. This meant that, for huge numbers of the group, there was a sigh of relief that they wouldn't have been reprimanded or scolded for not being behind. It implied these individuals cheerfully came, after quite a long time after month achieving solely under their objective, and as long as they did what's needed to be in the green, they inclined that they were doing fine. For those in the group who hit 100%, and again these would, in general, be the particular case as opposed to the standard, there was an odd feeling of selling out.

The individuals in the group who were achieving what was being asked of them felt like they were not getting the acknowledgment for really hitting the set out objective. Sure they were getting more commission and subsequently more cash. Yet, in group gatherings, they regularly commented that the honors and congrats were loaded similarly on the individuals hitting just underneath the figures as the individuals who were doing that 10 – 20 percent more and meeting or surpassing what was asked of them.

At the point when this group previously began, there wasn't a lot of grumbling. The desires were extreme, and the item they were being approached to sell was a difficult one, which required specialized skill. Just as the capacity to truly show clients and organizations how they would get value from it, so in the first place, there was a feeling that is given a polite gesture for getting nine-tenths of the route there was a massive achievement. The issue emerged when this was not clarified plainly. It ought to have been made understood from the start that this acknowledgment of not achieving was an impermanent status while everybody got up to speed, sadly it remained months after the fact, and new individuals to the group were urged to focus on 80% instead of the full 100.

Because of this, there started a distinction. Those hitting the appointed figures felt like they weren't getting enough prize and acknowledgment, though others thought that they could drift by at 4/5 of what they were being requested. Individuals are beginning backing off towards the month's end. As opposed to, which occurs in many associations, there is a significant drive toward the finish of the business period to make the objectives or achieve the goals. If somebody were agreeable in speculation, they'd end the month on 80%; they essentially quit placing in the exertion. This was soon to have a knock-on impact, and when the objectives were reexamined upwards a few months after the fact, individuals felt like they were impossible. The truth was they had made them that route independent from anyone else imposing a limit.

I have a strange analogy for you about approaching the finish of your objectives. Have you, at any point, had a massive variety of shopping sacks to convey home? A large portion of us eventually have. There's an unusual thing our psyche does. Regardless of how heavy the bags are, or how far our home is from the shop, we are pre-wired to achieve something fascinating. At the point when we see the end in locating, be it our entryway or our front entryway, this is the point at which our arms begin to hurt, and this is when everything feels a lot heavier. Why would that be? The simple answer is that we program ourselves to feel a liberating sensation when we see the end in locating as opposed to when we've achieved it. On school sports days I was a genuinely good runner, yet

I regularly came next, third, or more terrible because I backed off as I moved toward the end goal.

If you wind up doing this, don't stress, you're not the only one. This is a typical issue that faces sales reps, and not merely in deals. We appear to experience the ill effects of a similar burden at whatever point we are given a race to run or an objective to achieve. The appropriate response when you consider it is fundamental. We have to point past the target. OK, this may seem like a conspicuous articulation; however, it requires another degree of order and a perspective on that contentions with a great deal of the manners in which we regularly get things done. For instance, if we work in a business group and are given an objective of 100 offers of an item or service for a particular period, we have to compellingly advise our brains to clear out the number 100 and substitute with something like 120. I'm not saying we need to hit this new discretionary number, what I am stating is by focusing on that we should at present be hitting 100 at max throttle. This is the primary concern; we shouldn't back off as we approach our end game. We ought to control through it at full power and if we hit 120 fantastic! Shows we can do it, and more than that, when the goal lines move, as they do, we're increasingly arranged to go the additional separation as opposed to going after for this new target as of now on the back foot.

CHAPTER 10
LAW OF 3

Do you experience difficulty organizing every one of the things you have to complete? Stress never again! Follow the "Rule of Three" for better time management of everything you need to complete.

Regardless of what number of various things you do in a week or a month, there are just three tasks and exercises that record for 90% of the estimation of the commitment you make to your business. This is known as the "Rule of Three."

Make a List

If you make a rundown of all that you do over a month, it will most likely incorporate 20, 30, or even 40 different tasks and responsibilities.

If you audit your list carefully, thing by thing, you will locate that lone three things on your whole list represent

90% of your value to your business.

The Three Magic Questions

How would you decide your "huge three"? Basic. Make a list of ALL your work tasks and duties, from the first day of the month to the most recent day, and consistently. At that point, answer these three magic questions.

1) If I could do one thing on this list throughout the day, which one action would contribute the highest value to my business? You're most significant task in the Rule of Three – one that records for the best commitment you can make to your business – will presumably jump out at you when you make a list. It will, as a rule, be very obvious to you, as it is evident to the individuals around you. Put a hover around that thing.

2) If I could do two things on this list throughout the day, what might be the second action that would make the most significant contribution to my business? For the most part, this thing will leap out at you too. It might require somewhat more ideas, yet it is generally clear and self-evident.

3) If I could do three things on this list throughout the day, what might be the third movement that would contribute the most value to my business? At the point when you make a list and break down your answers, you will unmistakably observe that lone three things you do represent practically the entirety of the worth that you contribute. Beginning and finishing these tasks is a higher priority than everything else you do.

Don't Waste Time

Important Tip: If you don't have the foggiest idea about the responses to these three inquiries, you are in a tough situation. You are at a significant risk of wasting your time and wasting your life at work. If you do not know the answers to the Rule of Three inquiries, you will consistently wind up chipping away at the lower-level worth and frequently no-value exercises.

At the point when you can perceive what three tasks represent 90% of your worth, it resembles everything else you are doing fades away. Different tasks can be designated, done later, or not done by any means. Time the board will be a lot simpler because you will know what you are going after and the worth that you are contributing.

Make a move!

If you are unclear in any way, shape, or form, ask your chief. Ask what your manager believes are the most significant things that you do to make your most crucial commitment at work. Ask your coworkers. Ask your life partner. Be that as it may, whatever you do, you should know the responses to the Rule of Three.

Before you start work for the afternoon, set aside some effort to think gradually, make a list, select your most significant task, and afterward begin dealing with that assignment to the avoidance of everything else. Time the executives begin with you having the option to make a list and distinguishing your top tasks.

Mark Twain once said that if the principal thing you do every morning is to eat a live frog, you can experience the day with the fulfillment of realizing that that is presumably the most noticeably worst thing that will transpire throughout the day. Your "frog" is your highest, most significant task, the one you are well on the way to delay if you don't take care of business.

If You Have To Eat Two Frogs, Eat the Ugliest One First

This is another method for saying that if you have two significant errands before you start with the most exceptional, hardest, and most significant assignment first. Train yourself to start quickly and afterward to continue until the task is finished before you go on to something different.

If You Have To Eat A Live Frog At All, It Doesn't Pay To Sit and Look At It For Very Long

The way to arriving at elevated levels of execution and profitability is to build up the deep-rooted propensity for handling your significant assignment first thing every morning. You should build up the daily practice of "eating your frog" before you do whatever else and without setting aside an excess of effort to consider it.

This habit is well-received among successful individuals, to such an extent that I think of it as a central authority quality for any CEO, which means to achieve incredible things.

Take Action Immediately

Successful, productive people are the individuals who dispatch legitimately into their significant tasks and afterward train themselves to work relentlessly and resolutely until those tasks are complete.

"Failure to execute" is perhaps the most concerning issue in associations today. Numerous individuals mistake movement for achievement. They continuously talk, hold unlimited groups, and make brilliant arrangements; however, in the last investigation, nobody carries out the responsibility and gets the outcomes required.

For instance, if you have ever longed for turning into a distributed creator to propel your vocation, develop your business, or to improve the lives of others, none of those things will occur until you change your craving from fantasy to an objective. Indeed, even by then, despite everything, you have to make a move right away.

Develop a Positive Addiction

You can build up a "positive addiction" to endorphins and to the feeling of upgraded clarity, certainty, and skill that they trigger.

At the point when you build up this dependence, you will, at an oblivious level, start to compose your life so that you are continually beginning and finishing perpetually significant tasks and projects. You will get dependent, in an extremely positive sense, to progress and commitment.

No Shortcuts

The practice is the way to acing any ability. Luckily, your psyche resembles a muscle. It becomes more grounded and progressively fit with the use. With training, you can gain proficiency with any behavior or develop any habit that you think about, either attractive or important.

What is your "frog?" What is the one assignment that you despise doing every day? When you have picked your "frog," make it a propensity to get up each morning and carry out that responsibility first.

The best work habit you can ever get into is basic: Do your most exceedingly lousy assignment before anything else. Each given day, you have one significant to-do that is the highest need. However, when you have the entire day loosening up in front of you, it's anything but challenging to postpone it until after you get your espresso, browse our email, or go to that gathering. In any case, much the same as breakfast is the most significant dinner of the day, the primary thing you achieve at work establishes the pace for the remainder of the day.

Do your most exceedingly awful task first. By "worst," I signify "generally significant," and by "generally significant," I mean the task you're destined to stall on. The cutoff time you're fearing, the slides for the introduction you're scared of giving, the examination you're sure will turn up data you would prefer not to know. Do it before you do whatever else before you have the opportunity to consider it to an extreme.

Creator Brian Tracy calls this "eating your frog," citing Mark Twain. Twain broadly said that if the principal thing you do in the first part of the day is to eat a live frog, you can experience the remainder of the day, realizing the most noticeably terrible is behind you. Your frog is your most noticeably worst task, and you ought to do it before anything else.

Before anything else, your brain is clear, the workplace is calm, and you haven't gotten pulled into six different bearings yet. It's your one chance to organize what makes a difference to you most before your telephone begins ringing and email inbox starts dinging. By taking out something significant on your daily agenda before whatever else, you get both energy and a feeling of achievement before 10 AM.

Set yourself up to eat your frog tomorrow first thing last thing before you leave the workplace this evening. Pick your frog, and record it on a bit of paper that you'll see when you land back at your work area toward the beginning of the day. On the off chance that you can assemble the material, you'll have to complete it and have that out, as well.

Completing things is a propensity, and if you start each day by achieving something significant, you'll accomplish over 90% of the individuals in the workplace.

CHAPTER 11
TIME IS LIKE CAPITAL; YOU CAN'T LET SOMEONE STEAL YOUR SEED COIN

How to Prioritize Tasks

85% of American's concede they don't have the foggiest idea how to organize just as they might want.

- How do you feel about the issue?

- Do you ever feel overpowered by the measure of work you have?

- Have you, at any point, missed a significant cutoff time?

- Or neglected to achieve something significant?

That is alright, and I have an answer for you.

These are side effects of unpolished time management skills. You should refine your prioritization abilities and start (or come back) to productively evaluate your tasks with a legitimate plan for the day.

Sounds simple, isn't that so?

However, heaps of individuals will, in general, be amazed when I notice there's more than one type of to-do list.

Plan for the day is vital for proficiency since they list everything that you need to do, the most significant tasks at the top, and the least significant tasks at the bottom.

Influence Your Organizational Skills

Your capacity to improve your hierarchical abilities and prioritize tasks is a proportion of your general skill. The better the arrangement you have, regardless of whether as basic as making a to-do list, the simpler it is for you to overcome procrastination and begin to eat that frog and continue onward.

One of your top goals at work ought to be for you to prioritize tasks by utilizing your authoritative abilities to get the most elevated conceivable profit for your speculation of mental, passionate, and physical energy.

Create Your To-Do List

Set your organizational skills to work and organize errands by continually working from a list. When something new comes up, add it to the list before you do it. By realizing how to organize tasks, you can build your profitability and yield by 25% or more from the first day that you start working reliably from a list.

Having such a framework set up will make it a lot simpler to achieve all that you want – particularly long-term objectives, for example, composing a book.

Improve your organizational skills and make out your daily agenda the previous night, toward the finish of the workday. Move everything that you have not yet achieved onto your to-do list for the coming day and afterward add everything that you need to do the following day.

Time Management Tools

Regularly you will wake up with extraordinary thoughts and bits of knowledge that you can organize errands and use to complete your activity quicker and superior to anything you had at first idea.

The additional time you take to make written lists of all that you need to do, ahead of time, the more viable and productive you will be our 4 Master Lists

There are four different lists that you have to make for various purposes to improve your organizational skills and deal with your time.

1) First, you should make a master list on which you record all that you can think about what you need to do sooner or later. This is where you catch each thought that comes to or each new assignment or duty that surfaces. You would then be able to organize tasks more subsequently.

2) Second, you should have a month to month list that you make up toward the month's end for the month ahead. This may contain things moved from your lord list.

3) Third, you ought to have a week after week list where you plan your whole week ahead of time. This is a rundown that is under development as you experience the present week.

4) Finally, you move things from your month to month and week by week records onto your day by day list.

Organize Tasks For Ultimate Efficiency

At the point when you have a task of any sort, start utilizing your authoritative skills by making a to-do list of each progression that you should finish to complete the venture from start to finish. Prioritize tasks by organizing the project by priority and sequence.

Spread it out before you on paper or a PC with the goal that you can see it. At that point, get down to business on each errand in turn. You will be stunned at the amount you complete like this.

Recall that the Pareto Principle, otherwise called the 80/20 Rule, says that 20% of your effort will, in general, produce 80% of your outcomes, so organizing is an unquestionable requirement.

To identify your priorities, you have to know the contrast between what is essential and what is superfluous, says Tim Elmore, creator of Marching off the Map and leader of Growing Leaders, a nonprofit leadership training and advancement association. "Most leaders start well, yet in the long run, simply respond to what others need," he says. "We center on traversing the week as opposed to preparing and arriving at an objective."

Realizing your needs move you from being receptive to proactive. Three questions can assist you with deciding your most noteworthy needs, says Elmore:

1. What is expected of me in this job? Identify basic tasks and targets you've been given in your position, taking note of what must complete because it's a fundamental piece of the activity.

2. What produces the best outcomes when I do it? List the exercises you do that outcome in the most organic product; practices where individuals concur that you're very good at that task.

3. What is most satisfying when I do it? As you reflect on your projects and tasks, note which ones are profoundly fulfilling. "What are the tasks that you love and would appreciate, regardless of whether you weren't paid?" Elmore asks.

LIVING YOUR PRIORITIES

To live as indicated by your priorities, make a

timetable that puts them at the bleeding edge. Make a to-do list each day with deadlines, and set needs by giving a number to each assignment on your list, putting the most significant things first, Elmore recommends. "It's not fun things first, quick things first, or simple things first, yet first of all," he says.

Manage interruptions by placing edges in your schedule for startling individuals; however, don't get occupied, includes Elmore. Question everything: "Don't let sacred cows keep you from eliminating unnecessary or unproductive tasks," he says. "Focus on greatness, not perfection. Attempting to be immaculate can prevent progress."

Adjusting PERSONAL PRIORITIES

For a considerable lot of us, our actual needs are close to home, for example, family, says Clayton. "At the point when somebody is worried about whether they have put a sufficiently high need on family, I ask them for what good reason they work," he says. "A greater number of times than not, the appropriate responses I hear are that individuals work to have a greater or more pleasant house or to take extremely decent get-away. The appropriate responses will, in general, return to family, however, are established in materialism."

While there's nothing amiss with attempting to procure cash to purchase pleasant things, it's essential to acknowledge how a lot of time with your family you're surrendering to gain some money for anything that they're working for, says Clayton. "The 'a-ha' minute for some is that they're working extended periods organizing work while disregarding what they thought was the need from the beginning," he says.

To make family a genuine need, think about taking on a job at work that requires less time and energy, saving time for family, recommends Clayton. "All things considered, there's a 99.999% possibility this will lead to reduced income," he says. "That makes this choice for organizing family an intense pill to swallow." To start with, answer the question: Is everything extremely significant?

Regardless of whether everything on your plate should be similarly significant, despite everything, you need an approach to separate which ones you invest your energy in and how you cut up your time. The principal question you need to move beyond is whether everything truly is of equivalent significance. Here are several hints to assist you with slicing through the mist and discover how significant your obligations and projects genuinely are.

Grill the boss

At work, you have an administrator. At home, you're your chief. One of the essential obligations of any leader is to enable you to understand what's significant, what's not, and what you ought to be dealing with. You may have a supervisor at the workplace who does this (or necessities your assistance doing it well). Yet, wherever else, you're accountable for your work, and nobody's going to reveal to you that support up your information is more significant right now than painting the house. It's anything but difficult to surrender and believe "it's immensely significant," yet at work, you can lean in and tell your manager that you truly need their assistance. At home, at times, you need to pick something from your plan for the day and begin to gather some momentum.

Ask around

If you're prioritizing tasks that include others, similar to your family, companions, and collaborators, converse with them. Discover from them when they need your assistance, how much work is sponsored up behind the things you're working with them on, and if they can assist. If they needn't bother with you for one more week and another person requires you tomorrow, or if they aren't as occupied as you seem to be, you recognize what to do.

Work backward

We'll get into this somewhat later. However, you presumably have thought of when every one of your tasks is expected or if nothing else when you'd as them done by and how much time is required to take a shot at everything. Start with the due dates, consider how much effort you have to place into everyone and how much information you need from others. Work in reverse to discover what you ought to be chipping away at the present moment (or what you ought to have just begun, now and again).

Keep yourself responsible

At long last, when you've set aside some effort to figure out what's extremely significant and masterminded them dependent on what you figure you should handle first, it's an ideal opportunity to state it and offer it with everybody included expressly. Set desires with others for when you'll complete your work for them, and set wishes with yourself for when you'll have the opportunity to take a shot at your very own projects. This is progressively significant in a work setting, but involving others in your non-work to-dos can also keep you—and others—accountable.

Get organized

For your priorities to even matter, you have to have a type of an individual efficiency framework set up to which you consider yourself responsible and in which your needs will matter. If you have a proven framework, fantastic. If not, look at our manual for building one that is directly for you.

The objective of your framework, whichever you

select, is to remove the requirement for you to sit around choosing what to deal with directly, in any event, when you have a ton on your plate. I've discovered that David Allen's GTD structure is one of the best strategies for me, for the most part since it centers on what you ought to do now and what your next activities ought to be, and it stresses getting your to-dos out of your head and into some framework that will enable you to work. There are a lot of different alternatives, as recently referenced Wunder list, or if you chip away at a group, Asana, shared tools we love.

Whichever tools and efficiency technique you pick, dump your to-dos and tasks into it as fast as could be expected under the circumstances. Ensure it's something you'll really come back to and use now and again, and something that is anything but difficult to fit into your work process, and you'll be successful. At last, you need something simple to allude to, simple to enter tasks into, and that gives you an extraordinary perspective on the entirety of the balls you have noticed all around whenever.

View, the trinity: cost, degree and time

At the point when I was a project manager, one of the main things I figured out how to assist me with making a decision about which projects were generally significant or required the most consideration is the "triple constraint" or a triangle with three symmetrical sides. Each side speaks to the expense of the task, the extent of the job, and the time required to finish the project. None of the parties can be balanced without making changes to the next different sides. The sides you're weakest in helping decide the projects that need unique consideration. This remains constant for all things, not merely projects and task directors: If somebody piles more work onto you (scope), yet demands that you finish in a similar measure of (time), you'll need more assets (cost) to take care of business.

For instance, if you need to paint the extra room in time for away visitors to remain over, you can't change the size of the activity (scope). Yet, you can control whether you lock in and do it without anyone else's help medium-term (time), or get another person to do it for you while you achieve something different (cost). Here's how you can utilize these three standards to write your ordinary to-dos.

Time: Work in reverse from your cutoff times

Time is typically the one variable; the more significant part of us can't change. Deadlines are deadlines, and regularly we're not the ones who set them. This is the place working in reverse from due dates is essential. Start a spreadsheet and discount when each task or assignment on your plate should be done. At that point, work in reverse to the present day, considering everything every particular to-do that should be done to get from here to there, and to what extent it takes to finish. At the point when you're done, you'll likely observe a lot of tasks that ought to have begun as of now and others that ideally won't begin for some time in case you're going to make the deadline. That list, without anyone else, is a decent pointer of what your needs are. What you should be working on right now, what you should work on next, and perhaps most importantly, what you ought to find support with, particularly if they're tasks that ought to have begun seven days prior.

Cost: Get help from family, companions, and associates

Cost implies something beyond dollars. It also means individuals who can support you or services you can call to give you a hand or take the heap off. Might you be able to complete quicker if another person dealt with it for you? Imagine a scenario in which a colleague could accept some portion of the position off your hands, and you could get it later. Maybe there's a program or application that can automate the procedure for you, and it's pretty cheap. It might merit going through cash or dragging in companions to assist you with wrapping up the kitchen before you come up short on an extended get-away day, or calling somebody to introduce your new clothes washer, so you don't need to go on vacation to do it.

Delegate, delegate, delegate

It's simple for us to toil away in lack of definition, quietly hating our lives and our employments and developing frustrated as time passes. At the same time, there might be a companion who will help if we had just asked, or a manager who would assist you with excursion if you posed the right questions or gave them the accurate data.

We've discussed how tough it very well may be to delegate, and how to assign adequately previously, yet anyway you go about it, recall that you should be confident, not forceful when requesting help, and you have to put forth your defense with the entirety of the information you have accessible. At this point, you ought to have your needs spread out, and you have a smart thought of what you need. Utilize that data to request help and demonstrate you need it, and recollect, don't be disturbed if your companions, chief, or colleagues state no.

Buckle up—it's going to be a bumpy ride

Utilizing this strategy to set your own needs and monitor your very own obligations isn't merely something you ought to do when you're beginning to feel overwhelmed. If the walls are surrounding you, indeed, it's unquestionably time to take a decent, hard take a gander at what's on your plate, what can fall off, and what needs to give. However, holding up until you're as of now occupied and worried will make it particularly hard to roll out the improvements you have to get your head above water. All things being equal, it's fundamental, and once you do it, you'll never think back.

CONCLUSION:

In conclusion, time management is a significant ability to be scholarly and to be mastered to have a preferred way of life. By managing a great time, you will never again experience the ill effects of pressure, and your works/tasks will be done on schedule and with incredible quality. Remember that it is critical to have the attitude to change your timetables and to change procrastination. Also, consider the entirety of the clarified systems that are exceptionally useful to achieve a superior time for the executives. It is important to include that sports additionally give a supportive hand to time management, and grant your body to be sound and to have a superior group of friends. Regularly, people take time management programs so they can build a number of things that they can do on an everyday premise. Nonetheless, as the wise man stated, "There is a whole other world to life than just speeding up." The primary reason for learning and practicing time management skills is to upgrade and improve the general nature of your life. It is to build the measure of delight and happiness you experience. What we gain from the time the board isn't additional time yet a superior life. At the point when you figure out how to utilize viably the time that is given to you, you can have additional time with your family, avoid getting worried, improve your degree of profitability and be progressively successful in achieving your goals. Time the board is a craftsmanship in itself that incorporates arranging, organizing, scheduling, and budgeting time. This causes us to become progressively beneficial and productive at work, school, and every single other movement. We have seen that time the executives can be practiced by arranging, organizing, and sorting out your exercises. The list of individuals who can profit by the better time the executives is a long one and includes students, teachers, factory workers, managers, business owners, artists, musicians, contractors, engineers, clergy, and countless others. The truth of the matter is, about everybody can profit by learning the standards and systems of how to be better stewards of time. Build up the propensity for making the best choice at the correct time. Work done at an inappropriate time isn't very useful. Try not to squander a total day on something which should be possible in an hour or so.

Also, keep some time separate for your calls or checking reports on Facebook or Twitter. After all, a person isn't a machine. Throw what all you don't need. Toss what everything you needn't bother with. Put significant archives in envelopes. Keep the documents in their particular drawers with names over each record. It spares time, which goes on pointless looking. Time is important, truth be told, time is more significant than cash. Time is significant somewhat for the explanation that we are, for the most part, just allotted a specific amount of time in our lives; thus, we have to ensure that we use it wisely. Nothing can stop the progression of time. Time once past can't be brought back using any means. In any case, a few people don't understand the estimation of time and misspend it. Rather than concentrating on significant jobs needing to be done, they burn through their time, imagining that they would make up the loss in the future. They ought to understand that a large number of things to come inconveniences can be dodged by making a brief move on time. Time-management consistently remains the basic achievement factor. If anybody wastes his youth, he won't have the option to secure and develop character in the future and will endure all outcomes. Also, if an understudy disregards his investigations from every day, no measure of hard work before the assessment will get him through. Time-management is a decent propensity and establishes the framework of achievement in the future. It is significant to do like a lot of good as we can in a lifetime. An individual who understands the significance of time work in an efficient way. The more effectively we act, the additional time we will have leftover for future activities. If we look all around significant occasions of history, we will see that every single fruitful individual of history utilized time. The prosperous individuals of the world are aware of the estimation of the time. Subsequently, we should never burn through our time and attempt to utilize it. If time goes out, it doesn't return. We waste time unnecessarily. But, we don't utilize it well. So we have bombed a great deal. If we need to defeat the disappointment, we need to pick time management. But some have to work hard. If you buckle down, the outcomes will be vastly improved. Research charge on time the executives. Find new things. Guarantees that the entire life will be alive with time management. With the goal that you can go to a generally excellent level throughout everyday life. You can make this progress after one achievement. With the goal that your life is so excellent.

www.ingramcontent.com/pod-product-compliance
Lightning Source LLC
Chambersburg PA
CBHW060831220526
45466CB00003B/1065